Also by Daniel Halpern

POETRY

Traveling on Credit
The Lady Knife-Thrower
Street Fire
Life Among Others
Seasonal Rights
Tango
Foreign Neon

TRANSLATIONS

The Songs of Mririda, by Mririda n'Aït Attik
Orchard Lamps, by Ivan Drach (co-translator)

EDITOR

Borges on Writing (co-editor)
The American Poetry Anthology
The Antaeus Anthology
The Art of the Tale:
An International Anthology of Short Stories
On Nature
Writers on Artists
Reading the Fights (co-editor)
Plays in One Act
Our Private Lives: Journals, Notebooks, and Diaries
The Sophisticated Cat (co-editor)
Not for Bread Alone:
Writers on Food, Wine, and the Art of Eating
The Autobiographical Eye

SELECTED POEMS

SELECTED POEMS

Daniel Halpern

ALFRED A. KNOPF NEW YORK 1994

THIS IS A BORZOI BOOK
PUBLISHED BY ALFRED A. KNOPF, INC.

Library of Congress Cataloging-in-Publication Data

Halpern, Daniel.
  [Poems. Selections]
  Selected poems / Daniel Halpern. — 1st ed.
    p. cm.
  ISBN 0–679–42986–7
  I. Title.
PS3558.A397A6 1994
811'.54—dc20

93–33368
CIP

Manufactured in the United States of America
First Edition

FOR JEANNE AND LILY

CONTENTS

I

TRAVELING ON CREDIT

II

STREET FIRE

III

LIFE AMONG OTHERS

IV

SEASONAL RIGHTS

V

TANGO

VI

FOREIGN NEON

[I]

TRAVELING ON
CREDIT

THE ETHNIC LIFE

I've been after the exotic
For years: champac
And patchouli in air, distant
Root scents, their smoke
Dazing rooms where dark men
Sit on legs
On rugs.

I ride teak trains
Through the Khyber Pass
Into Pakistan, and speak
Tongues I can't write.

My wife is young,
She turns to me from the East
After prayer—
Her black hair, her
Eurasian face spreading
Below the long eyes
Like Asian night itself.

On summer evenings before the monsoon
I meet my contortionist
Lover from India
Over Campari.
In her room my eyes roll
To paradise, click
Like a pair of Moroccan dice;
The undoing of her spine
Releases me from mine.

In my life
There is no room
For bikinis or Chanel,
Or the waxed beauty of the West. . . .

For years I've lived simply,
Without luxury—
With the soundness of the backward
Where the senses can be heard.

[FROM *Traveling on Credit*]

THE GRASSHOPPER

Mokhtar sat in his favorite café on the Rue de la Plage and smoked his *kif*. As the old countrywomen passed with their vegetables he lighted pipe after pipe. When the last of his tea was finally gone, he got up and walked down to the Avenue d'Espagne, where he came upon a grasshopper eating an onion. He got down on his hands and knees to have a closer look and noticed that tears were coming from the grasshopper's eyes. The onion got smaller and smaller as the tiny mandibles worked around it like spider legs. Mokhtar stared, and the grasshopper kept on eating and weeping until the onion was gone.

SPRING ZOO

The children are too kind this year:
They've come to feed the mammals.
On the other side of glass
Snakes stretch their single extremity;
The baboons this season are as large as apes.

I watch the charges of *au pair* girls
Race the railing
For the elephants. On my bench
Down near the pond that's piled with seals
I share the fever, a jungle
Inmate of my own fantasy. The girls
Turn from sex to birds, or a hippo
Too vague to reproduce.

This year the children are just too kind:
They smile back at snakes or shake
An elephant's trunk.
The animals that are moving
Are unmoved by the round faces smiling
On the other side of steel. I feel Africa
Shiver in the trees, the children
And their attendants, the coupling
In cages. Having paid admission
I sit where the seals slide on moss

And let the big cats do my pacing.

[FROM *Traveling on Credit*]

DUTCH APRIL

Tulips charge the grazing dikes, and I walk
In wood along canals, the water
Creeping from street to street where old men talk
Herring days. The breath of every flower
Hangs a scent on the air like laundry,
Each color boxed with its pedigree
Nailed against the wind. These colors recur
Like familiar faces on wine evenings.

A tulip Sunday: dresses are wings
Beating beyond my reach. In the sweet wake
The fish women swoon in their reverse make-
Up, hawking sardines fresh from the North Sea.

A lighter, poled from still water, springs
Its load of ripe Edam upon the quay.

ARRIVING

On a day long and wet we fall upon
The city like tramps belched from all-night bus
Depots. Time is porcelain on the wall
As we step into the light. I will call
To the taxi stalling for his crude pay
Outside a bar, and if he comes for us
We will doze through falling streets, moving on
Until the heights break down before the bay.

At Steele's Motel a man behind a sign
Yawns his questions at us in hot clouds
And hands us a key, pointing where the night
Spills a crowd of different throats near a pine.
The cabin is a bed and desk—a shroud
Of moth wings on the screen, starving for light.

[FROM *Traveling on Credit*]

SHELDON'S POEM I

after Aleister Crowley

Sheldon put on his female garb
And called himself the Lesbian Dandy.
He needed to laugh at the limits,
Push back boundaries and move where the air
Was asexual. He left New York
And his city life for the grass-
Lands of the West. He had North Beach friends
Where Broadway rubbed against Chinatown.
The twist was already the craze
In the expensive clubs. Sheldon spent time
Off Market, cruising sailors from Asia
On leave with an erection and some dollars
To soften it. The girls were fucking
Beats and Haight hadn't started up yet.

SHELDON'S POEM II

The café sags out beneath a meager
Façade. Sheldon feeds us lines from New York
And the crowd slides by. I must say I prefer
This table where the wine sits without a cork.
Sheldon says, "A lot of chicks in velvet
Dresses won't talk to you if you look like
A creep," and goes on to the ethics
Of fountain pens. His eyes swim as the wine ticks
In his head. The sun nods on a hill like
A hand, and we move on to *espresso*.

My friend flaps in the small wind—she is high
And the day's words dance in her calico
Hair. Her smile squats in the street near a fly
As Sheldon starts himself up again, spill-
Ing his life as the sun enters the hill.

[FROM *Traveling on Credit*]

TRAVELING ON CREDIT

They would think up trips on Sundays—
Traveling to Lahore via Persia,
Sliding through the Khyber Pass,
Dropping into India like Polo.

The trips began off Fire Island
On a beach day with high red winds,
Swimming nude in South Bay
Together. The residents looked away,

Cared for their gardens which suffered
From the whip of the salt wind
And the Patchogians, who
Came with bayberry sandwiches

To hawk their bodies in the sun
And hurry back on the last
Watch Hill ferry. They lived
In Bayberry and thought up trips

With the marina's population
(A Calcutta of boats)
Looking on from polished wood.
They were, for the most part, in love,

Traveling, Sundays, to Lahore
In three cars with two wolfhounds,
Four afghans and a setter—
A Packard, a Daimler and a Ford.

They were set on Lahore:
Stops in Izmir and Isfahan,
The long crawl through Persia.
On Sundays, in fine weather,

They set out with a pocketful
Of visas and rolled east, content
With itineraries of sand
And postcards back on the weekend.

[FROM *Traveling on Credit*]

PINK SHARON

Pink Sharon
Is the lipstick in her purse.
I look to her feet
And in my head fasten my hand
To her ankle.

They said, "If you can't
Put your hand round a girl's ankle
Don't marry her," and I've been spanning
Ankles for years.

She sits next to me on the train
And rattles her purse—
I see the Pink Sharon,
The small ankles,
And drop a coin. I bend for it,
My hand falling to her ankle,
My fingers finding each other,

And I look into her eyes
And she looks into mine,

And I say, yes—
And between my fingers
She says, yes.

FROG NIGHTS

The frogs outside my window hog the night—
Their sound is of a certain art
That has wandered beyond the tight
Beat from a polyrhythmic heart.

I turn you over and move
From a favorite direction,
Sending you to that teeming pond
Where nothing is left undone.

And there is no need to disprove
These various ways we grow fond,
In a night, of things that respond.

The black is pregnant with croaking
And different loves just beyond
This room, where in disguise we move.

[FROM *Traveling on Credit*]

WOMEN

She dreams
Smooth green snakes
On rainy nights

It seems
He read her
Rough copies of great poems

She would fake
Understanding so he
Could go to bed happy

She thought it right
Things went on this way
For he brought home

Beautiful things from the city

PASTIMES

"Why, you're a genius," she said.

A natural enough comment I thought
As I glued a side to my plane
And started papering the fuselage.

I could see her on the couch,
Her hands clicking with needles and wool.

"Why, you're a genius," I said.

She nodded,
Thinking the remark natural enough
As she placed the last stitch in a sleeve.

It's not bad living with a genius
We both think
As we glue and stitch through life.

[FROM *Traveling on Credit*]

LIKE ANYONE

She had theories: like every eel
Going to the Sargasso Sea before dying.
Like salmon. Like Moslems.

Like doing minuets to calm down,
Or birds hating tilting houses.

Her house tilted and the birds stayed away—
Nuthatch, grosbeak, cardinal. . . .

She saw pigs as horses
When they were stranded, straddled
In the snow to their bellies,
And believed in white witches—
Males who predicted like crazy
While they danced and looked
Like anyone.

Like not washing her hair
To keep it full.
Like the wooden fish
She sucked for health.

Theories were her slaves,
And she was young with hair
White as witches.

The eels in her smokehouse
Hung from their chins near the bowl
Where wooden fish soaked in oil.

While her hair thinned the birds flew
By the tilt of her house,
Like her life at the slight angle
She lived it.

[FROM *Traveling on Credit*]

FOLLOWING IT DOWN

Think how you will follow it down
The road where a wheel spins empty
And the blue weeds turn on themselves
As the sun beats time against the sky.

Think how you will follow it down
To the banks of a jealous river
Which races winter only
And turns its back to the heat of summer.

And when it settles like a fly
On the hand of a clock ticking
Seconds, breathing into time,
Keep an eye free for the beast that flashes
Out of the cobalt balance.

PERVERTS

1.

A lonely little man.
He lives with a white cat
In a house too big
Since his wife left.

2.

I never thought much
About the creeps in the park,
The ones who come out with the night
To lurk in red socks behind the gladiolas
Planted by the city.
All they do is watch couples
Steal sex off the benches.
I've even seen them hang from trees
And gape at the tight skin
Of a young girl's face!

3.

Some girls leap
From his eyes like waves,
While others dive
Fathoms below his belt—
The place where insects
Move in his hand.

[FROM *Traveling on Credit*]

He almost lets them go as they jump,
But they return
Once out
To roll through the fingers
He keeps out of sight.

4.

Oh, he's patient all right,
Sitting on his bench,
Crossing one leg over the other,
The bones clicking under his chino trousers.

Girls walk by
With mothers for eyes.

He can wait.

FIVE RIDDLES

1.

Your digs neither rouse nor rib
Me; of your kind there isn't one
I couldn't put on,
Feel the whole thing was a cinch. Remember,
I've been saddled with more:
My very nature once carried existence—
I swung my blond hair
And felt the wind keep pace upon my chest.
Now I merely tamp impatience
Into unripe moons of dirt.
I may be foolish,
Lose my head now and then in a wind
Or champ at the bit heading home,
But nothing more—there are
Pleasures to consider: a wardrobe
That's admired and can excite
The deviant among you, or girls
Who dream of me, hot
To trot the landscapes of their dreams.
No, things are not bad—
I may very well be the only stud
Among many more dashing
To walk this earth upon his own good luck.

2.

With a body full of vertebrae,
Dark muscle,
The insect moves on a long

[FROM *Traveling on Credit*]

Slow curve, too fast for us to focus
On, too quick to stop in flight
For a moment
And register impression.

We hear the sound it starts
Up from, and see the room
It makes for itself alighting
Only. Its home is a shell
That's shed when life
Is over. —That
First and final trip alone
Is its funeral.

3.

It is my pulse
That is father
To all others,
My hands,
Sure and deft,
That shape men's lives.

I speak every tongue
Known to man,
And yet they learn
My language as children,
Learn that my demands
Are unending,
My rule, final.

My beat has kept me alive
Forever,
I've had a part in every history
Though you will find

No trace of me
Anywhere.

But I am everywhere
And nowhere—

And I have the final word.

4.

Your arms cover half
Of everything
We know, allow
The quiet pulse of our time
Together. It is
In your presence that owls hoot into blackness
While others sleep. We move within your dark
Skein—you allow us to face
The face of our ambitions,
Give us our secret smiles
That later become public.

I would venture to guess
That it was in your presence,
And perhaps because of it,
That we began in this world, which is half yours.

5.

I lurk in shadows,
Venture out, thin-legged,
In the dark.

[FROM *Traveling on Credit*]

It is true,
I am older than anything
I hide in,
My ancestors are found in stone.

Women hate me,
Wish
To be rid of me,
Though I would not think
Of touching them.

For hunger only
I stay here,
Hard, fast,
My name, in part,
Keeps their world alive.

[II]

STREET FIRE

STREET FIRE

It is past midnight in a thick fog when sirens
call us to the terrace.
We look down onto blossoms of bright fire
opening from manholes on Fifth Avenue.
There are men standing and smoking in rubber jackets
outside a garment-district café,
the lights fluttering, the fire
offering us its electric smoke.
In bare feet and robes—the cat
and dog at our feet—we hear
the heat pound tubes stuffed with wire.
And somewhere down there, under the softening blacktop,
the gas mains wait to take in the whole block.
We bring the two or three small relics of our lives,
the dog and cat, and the elevator to the street.
There is a cold wind and ice in the gutters.
There is the street's midnight population
leaning against the wall of Reverend Peale's Sunday church.
We note the taxis that deliver strangers
to watch with us as the street shrivels and begins
to flow around the manhole covers.
They are all there: men of the brigade, the police,
women from nearby hotels, their furred men,
the strangers from the city.
What we see is the tip of the iceberg,
they tell us—and underneath
the tubes alive with flames.
For an hour we watch from the corner—
in this weather tragedies are distant.
The elevator back up contains the momentary explosion
in the eye where disasters flare—
our section of New York, between the flowers and furs,

is full of bright red petals.
We reach the ninth floor and step into air
powdered with radiator heat.
The tiny, muffled beats of fire below the street
pant through the window an even pulse.
The dog moves into the living room where the fire is dying
on bricks. The cat takes the warm tiles
of the bathroom. We stand silently, listen
a few minutes, then move to each other.
Our own fire is watered by the conviction
that things are right. Later, we listen to the small puffs
of heat spit from the manhole outside, smell
the smoke from live wires
bound with rubber that smolders into morning.

RUBBER JUNCTION

I am a man who has watched the sun break down
upon the single mountain of our plain.
There are sparrows in the air, nothing more
save the dust of ten generations.

In the morning I collect wood for the fire.
In the afternoon the train arrives on time.
In the evening, on the long porch, I fill my pipe,
letting the blue smoke out evenly into the pink

light leaning into the shadows around the house.
The children here grow up and train out before
understanding the imperceptible finger
of time that tamps year into year,

the train with its faces, legs of centipedes crawling
through the sand, around our single mountain.
There is little, really, to say—
the dreams of the dead will take us in their hands

and shake us into a sleep of their own.
I know it is something not unknown to me
I see, watching the sun break down
behind the single mountain of our plain.

Perhaps one day, while I am collecting wood in the morning,
a dark cloud will spread itself on top of my armful of wood,
and I'll carry it, unsuspecting, into the house.
Later, when we've touched the roots of night,

lightning will burst through the halls,
thunder sounding through the bedrooms,
bringing us to our sleeping feet
as the flood begins a slow descent down the stairs.

[FROM *Street Fire*]

THE LANDING

Out here a woman wonders.
And if she has no man
her arms get strong.
—CAROLYN FORCHÉ

On the prow,
standing on red planks,
the white maiden holds
hand to temple,
faint, keening.
The fog snags the edge
of her gown, dissolves
it at the ankle, begins
for thighs, for breasts
unlike white stone, her
neck, and then her
lips like white stone.
She sees scrub dabbed
on a mountain, its peak
thrust through the layer of air-cloth.
There are sirens of anger in the air
that call to trees.
Wasps prowl the reef—
the maiden, kneeling now,
watches them,
watches parrot fish bite and snap
for food, lovers
of the vegetable, hanging in kelp beds.
And now, behind her,
behind wasp and siren,
the ship of women prisoners
begins to undo itself.
The fog,
the life's-breath in a cold

climate, lifts.
Their legs are thin and hard
from the voyage, they are wise
progeny of the white maiden
who moves their vessel
past wasps who have given way,
past parrot fish in kelp
with their bright colors
less brilliant than hers,
and onto the wave that rises,
lifts them, lifts them up
level with mountain scrub,
then down
through layers of water,
down to the soft fingers of sand
that are not their fathers
and yet,
and yet take them in.

[FROM *Street Fire*]

THE SISTERHOOD

If you let them, they'll take your eyes away,
knock out the sight-spot inside the color

on a stone and carry them off, blind, to the street
where they come from. They'll polish those balls

on rugs and wear them between their fine shoulders.
If they could see, they'd see you walking downtown

with a white stick or a dog. Your hands now are sockets.
Your arms thin chains hanging beyond the seat of your hips.

If you relax with sun-heat in your mouth near night,
they'll come up behind you and carry away your tongue.

You might have told them it didn't speak,
but now it's too late. They take it to their street

where they rub it down with the domestic oils
from their bodies. They're not glad to have it

when they discover it won't talk. They beat it
with the fiction of their mouths and bury it.

When the tongue, thick with the weight of earth
lifts into flower, it sings to your teeth

from the garden where they live.
You can hear it, but nothing more.

You didn't let them take your eyes away.
They stole your tongue that didn't speak

and beat it and buried it and wore your eyes.
The eyes are blind. You hear them clicking

on their chains outside your door.
You guess the rest is easy.

They unsheathe the knives of your fantasy.
They begin the long incision into sleep—

the blade runs for the eyes of your dream,
lifts you upon its edge to the waking street.

DEJA VU

The great wings of the fan spread
the air around the bed, the cat
pads through the hall after errant sound.

I awake in a fist of pale light
to touch you awake. I am dreaming
this moment that years from now

another will share
as he sits up in bed
next to you

and in your sleeping face
know that he has been here once,
but in another room—

he hears the swish
of an overhead fan and the cat
as it leaps for the sound

that brought him out of sleep.
When he touches you
it will be with my hands.

THE LADY KNIFE-THROWER

In the gay, silver air of the tent
I'm at ease, fingers
at rest in my lap.
Before me the tools of my trade—
cleaned, well oiled and waiting
for the warmth of my hand, for the time
when the flick of my wrist will send them
out into the morning for their casual trip
to my husband's waiting body.
One at a time they plant themselves at his sides,
tucking in the air around his body.

At night, under the big top,
he is strapped to the board.
With a roll of drums I appear with my knives
and release my repertoire of throws.

There is no question in our lives of fidelity.
At night, after the knives are cleaned and placed
in their teakwood rack, we are all we desire.

[FROM *Street Fire*]

THE BREAKER OF GLASS

It pleases him, how he multiplies
in the pool of glass he leaves
after his tiny hammer touches
telephone booths, lights of cars and windows.
He can feel himself freeze into pattern,
fall to pieces on the ground.
He hates what he breaks,
the smooth run of it on air.

Some men go for young girls,
the knuckles they've grown under their sweaters.
Others watch buildings fold up in flames.
He loves the pool of glass,
the cool sense of escape.
When the glass he's after is gone
he returns to his stone house,
lays the hammer on wood,
and looks deeply for himself
in the bathroom's dark wall.

SILENCE

—BELLA AKHMADULINA

Who was it that took away my voice?
The black wound he left in my throat
can't even cry.

March is at work under the snow
and the birds of my throat are dead,
their gardens turning into dictionaries.

I beg my lips to sing.
I beg the lips of the snowfall,
of the cliff and the bush to sing.

Between my lips, the round shape
of the air in my mouth.
Because I can say nothing,

I'll try anything
for the trees in the snow.
I breathe. I swing my arms. I lie.

From this sudden silence,
like death, that loved
the names of all words,
you raise me now in song.

[FROM *Street Fire*]

THE NEW BLAST-FURNACE IN THE
KEMEROVO METALLURGICAL COMBINE

—BELLA AKHMADULINA

Up there where the new blast-furnace rises
they are working.
A boy is laughing
as he balances in the wind.

Indifferently, he walks the thin ledge
and for a moment, just slightly,
tilts his head as if yearning
for the ground that awaits him.

He is at ease in the echo
of his erratic footfall,
in the scatter of sparks like fistfuls
of failing stars in an August sky.

Of course there is the bravado,
the passion and sudden expectation
that a passing girl will understand
the distance, his height above ground.

Girls have other things in mind—
one will look up, see him, and understand
nothing. It is something farther
that calls to her, something beyond him.

And yet, on a rare trip to the circus,
she will strain forward, pale
with concern for the walker
when he steps onto the wire.

With his anger cloaked, and almost cool,
he again looks down
onto the girls who have left him,
then scatters sparks, failing stars of fire.

GOD HASN'T MADE ROOM

—MRIRIDA N'AÏT ATTIK

My sister, you are a stranger to this place.
Why be surprised that I know nothing?
My eyes have never seen the rose.
My eyes have never seen the orange.
They say there is plenty down there
in the good country
where people and animals and plants are never cold.
My sister, stranger from the plains,
don't laugh at a barefoot girl from the mountains
who dresses in coarse wool.
In our fields and pastures
God hasn't made room for the orange.
God hasn't made room for the rose.
I have never left my village and its nut trees.
I know only the arbutus berries and red hawthorn,
and the leaves of green basil
that keep the mosquitoes away
when I fall asleep on the terrace
on a warm summer night.

THE INSULT

—MRIRIDA N'AÏT ATTIK

You are wrong, mother of my former husband,
if you think I am suffering.
You can tell your son who left me
that the good and bad days of our life together
are gone from my mind and heart,
just as straws scatter in the wind. . . .

I remember nothing of the work in the fields,
the loads that bruised my back,
the jugs that marked my shoulders,
my fingers, burned baking bread,
the bones he left me on festival days.

He took back the jewelry. Had he given it to me?
Did he beat me?
Did he take me in his arms?
I can't remember. . . .

It's as if I had never known him.

You who were my mother-in-law, go tell your son
that I no longer know his name!

[FROM *Street Fire*]

FEVER JOURNAL

12 JANUARY

It is evening. Purple
smoke rises from the fields:
they are burning the clothing
of the infected and the dead,
those few without fever.
It is evening and I am sitting
with tea, reading in the yellow light.

3 FEBRUARY

Today is Sunday. No bells.
Only the unwinding of the muezzins
over the valley, down to the river.
The steady pulse of drums is gone.

27 FEBRUARY

I awake in the night,
the warm hands of fever
at my temples. I imagine
this, the head
taking over my body,
flapping it out on the bed
like laundry upon the river.
I hear dogs moving in the street,
frogs breathing under the bridge.
My hands are cool.
There is light in the window.
I have survived another night.

3 MARCH

This morning birds
flew out of the smoke
heading north across the water.
I remain here with the fever,
without mail, with radio reports
that carry the news of Europe.

1 APRIL

The first day of Ramadan.
Rats move against the sunset
on electric wires into the trees.
The burning continues,
and I wait.

12 APRIL

Upon waking, I drink whiskey,
nap from noon till cannon's call.
I move to the dim light of a café.
There is little talk. The radio
blasts Egyptian film music.

27 APRIL

The smells of the marketplace
are lost. Smoke
is everywhere. Only a quick
trace of mint at afternoon tea.

[FROM *Street Fire*]

5 MAY

Today the sun is bright
and it has ended.

We have been marked by the fever.

And now it is evening—
I watch the last of the smoke
rise to meet the birds, moving
back over the water from the north.

THE SOLDIER

A soldier is walking in the streets of a very old city.
The women wear veils. The men are unfriendly.
The sun is not hot but there is dust
in sheets between every building.
He kicks the dogs that feed on his heels.
He pushes past crowds of children
whose hands are hats of loose change.

In its descent a kite drops to his head,
leaving a thin red line.
He picks up a chicken from a pile of seeds
and throws it at a wall.
A passerby asks, What has this chicken done to you?
The soldier replies, By God, a brother of his
left this mark on my head.
Yes, answers the passerby, but this is a domestic
chicken, and that was a wild kite.
Never mind, said the soldier.
They are birds, both this and that.

He leaves behind the walls of the city,
the veiled women, the begging dogs and children.
He walks in air free of dust and sound.

By midday he knows there will be no water
as the sun leans for him—
a bright bird out of the cobalt, like all the others.

[FROM *Street Fire*]

THE GIRL WHO DOESN'T SMILE

I am seated
in her immaculate salon,
my head cupped in the hand
of her private chair.
When she enters
I see immediately
that her passion is skin deep.
She puts her hand on my chin
and things begin: softly,
she slips her fingers
into my mouth, bending close,
her eyes to my eyes, her eyes
looking away. My elbow
gently rests against her stomach.
We are alone.

It's a strange girl who never smiles,
I think, a little on edge—
her serious face and tools
so pointed. I can see
she's not in this for fun,
yet does
find pleasure somewhere
in the pocket of my mouth.
And her fingers
bring tears to my eyes.
When it's over
she pulls her fingers from me

and I draw in my elbow.
She looks into my eyes at last
and I see there, in her triumph,
the passion that has kept from her
my own undying love.

[FROM *Street Fire*]

ENDINGS

1.

A few years later
(it was on a wet day),
 he was killed in an accident
 in the streets of Paris.
 She was terribly lonely
 and looked tired and broken,
 but she worked on.

2.

His speeches were short and sweet.
One of them ended,
If elected I shall be thankful.
If not, it will be all the same.

3.

And yet, none dare openly
love him.
That would have been undue indulgence
and bad for the boy.
So, what with scolding and chiding,
he became very much the stray dog
without a master.

4.

He was as much a stranger to the stars
as were his innocent customers,
yet he said things
that pleased and astonished everyone.
The note he left explained,
"That was more a matter of study,
practice, and shrewd guesswork."

5.

But now it is different.
I have lost everything.
Death is beautiful.
I will go tired and broken
when I have walked
three thousand times
round this floor.

[III]

LIFE AMONG
OTHERS

TAKE FOR EXAMPLE

Take the insect for example.
The pale wings that work in air
and the singing legs.

It goes forth into the air
unafraid. It can return
to the place it set out from,

or it can continue flying, outward.
If it does not turn back
it is always singing

to some new part of the world
as it passes—to the flower
in its first opening,

to the leaf floating on a branch,
to the bird upon the grass,
to the window and the house,

to the man who slaps the song
between his hands
in the one applause he knows.

And the man goes back.
He goes back to the place
he set out from without a song.

LIFE AMONG OTHERS

I tempt light off the bay till evening
moves across the hills and presses
into the city its engraver's ink. I won't say
why I'm here, or why I remain without moving
by day into the night. At the hotel
the lights in the other rooms go on one by one,
and in the garden, which overlooks the markets
of the old city, the palms flap, rooted
birds with green tropical wings.
The guests are at tangerines and Vichy
before the evening meal. While they eat
I sit in front of my window, I tempt
the solitary lights that go on and off
on the water: lights of boats, cape lights,
the lights across the water. They pile up
in darkness here. It is a collection, a pastime.
Now I have the chance to speak—not to explain
but to return everything—your bright lives
rooted to nothing more than a light seen at a distance
that diminishes as it moves closer and closer.
Where I am there is everything that is beautiful.
It is where I started out,
it is where I think of you now.
From this setting of props, I return it all.

PERSON SMOKING

Cigarette smoke floats up
to this second-story room.
It doesn't mean too much,
but it is a sensation.
Below me someone sits quietly.
There is no reason to believe
it is a woman, and there is no way
I can look out the window.
I imagine a woman sitting on a bench
smoking quietly, looking off
into the trees. I could of course
call out, but that would be ridiculous.
I wonder, as I stare into the trees,
what she is thinking about.
She can't know I'm here
and wouldn't care if she did.
She sits there as I sit here.
And then she laughs.
Startled, I turn back
into the room. She watches me
from the bed, smiling gently—
at what, I wonder.
Her cigarette is a gray ash that drops
into the white air of the sheets.

GLASSWORKS

You run out of invention and the glass stem
that holds the object snaps.
Nearly complete, the object rolls away
with the truth of completion still unformed.
What a sad life that uses the body
like this, to support what lives about it,
and make it live below intelligence.

[FROM *Life Among Others*]

LIME KILN

Late August, the dead days of lime
    bleaching clay near the kiln
        at Big Sur. I move forward

in shoes bleached by lime and sun,
    and in my face the stain
        of lime moving upon me.

The dead pots hump in corners
    around the shack. No music here
        but the music of white bone

drying beyond water in sun.
    Late August. I bring back distant
        summers—the air of memory,

the distal air of avatars
    mixing water and mud, clay,
        the admixture of sky and earth.

A few miles away the sea wind
    moves, sweeps salt in sheets over birds.
        I sit now on the gray wood

of the kiln's benches. It is bright.
    The salt, like birds hovering,
        moves on. I have never been here.

I'll leave no bones still pink with flesh
    or blood. There are no bones to leave.
        There are no thoughts to leave. Only

the mind runneled like earth, dry
    and bare as the limed earth,
        nothing but the wet flesh of memory.

[FROM *Life Among Others*]

BEGIN

We are in the room.
The light, the lizards on the screen
and the overhead fan are givens.
Now as we sit the light is going out.
Have you come to take what I say
to others? I say little:
the air that fills speech lies
in its chamber.
Light the candles—we will sit up tonight.
If you are quiet I will tell you.
I need only begin. Can you hear me?

STILL

I hear callers in the trees,
but I stay in one place,
knowing motion is nothing
if I can't stand like this
hour after hour.

In this immobility a fire inflates,
and so much turbulence within the static—
the owls call, still in their trees.
They can see in the night, they don't need to move.
I don't move myself—the river moves

somewhere, the clouds without sound
move and move. They drift and disband.
The dogs are still, except for their jaws,
which click in the night.
They smell the darkness, they don't need to move.

My work is to stand still and see everything.
My work is to rethink the immobile,
the owl and dog, and without moving release them,
release myself, let everything live again,
recalled into movement and loved, wholly still.

[FROM *Life Among Others*]

FOR YOU

You are not going to say any more now—
we are in bed and your fingers are closed
between your legs.
My hands are in their chambers.
We are talking with a low-watt bulb burning.
It is not sordid. It is raining.
There is unfriendliness between us
and your long white men's flannels.
For too long there has been cloth
between us.
                    Later the cat
will move down your length, a warm ball of fur
between us. My 800-pound arm
is sex, all man between us.
It is late. It is raining.
Others have conspired in this taking apart.
Objects have kept us
from each other.
In the front room there is an Eve all male.
The feeling here for you is all mine
and you are lost,
powerful, unsure—your angry renegade head. . . .
You are not sure.
I will find you
again and again.
You have held yourself against me.
You say,
This last long river is for you.

LETTER TO THE MIDWEST

You would notice the humor: storks
at work in the fields collecting seeds,
the pointing tips of *djellabas*
that stick up at odd angles—
closer to God, perhaps. The palms are dramatic,
waving wildly in wind. At their centers
the rust-colored fronds remain still.
You, of course, see the irony in this.
The rain stops and starts all day,
the horns left over from the Europeans'
New Year still sound in every street.
It's exotic all right.
It makes me gloomy and I imagine
snow fields without storks, corn instead of *kif*,
and little children off to school,
their hair lighter than snow,
speaking English, their mothers' kisses
still blossoming on their rosy cheeks.
But it's dusk here,
veiled figures go by outside my window,
the lights across the Strait begin to appear.
The bats have begun to feed, and the starlings,
in a frenzy, circle, and float home.

[FROM *Life Among Others*]

THE DANCE

No one's dancing here tonight.
Wouldn't you know it.
The cat in profile smiles at the light,
the rain is just a little sound on the metal
of the roof—out of season.

The cat doesn't dance and I wouldn't watch
if she did. Her little soul though
dances tonight, she is so pleased we are alone.
She smells the roast in the kitchen
and for my sake appreciates its progress.

There is a little fire burning: sawdust pressed
into a log and sold for a dollar keeps the light
the right tone and the heat up, although
it isn't really cold. No one is dancing,
the candles have been punched out,

and the amber has worn off the hardwood box.
Even the music, if it were playing, would make it
no different. Not even the rain or the food.
It doesn't matter little friend.
No one's dancing here tonight—wouldn't you know it.

BLUE SUSPENSION

Brown wood and moss-covering,
women, their wicker baskets

of dark bread and cold meats, wine
and the girl who wore the denim dress,

whose eyes I never saw in the strange
light of the afternoon. Take this

photograph from me, the lawn filled
with mallets and colored balls, wickets

and the trimmed hedge. I remember this,
the summer and the summer baskets, her dress

and the water when I found her, the strange
light on wood below the surface of water,

the dress fluttering there, fluttering
as if in a wind, as if I were seeing it

from the lawn, a dark wood scent still upon me,
the dry feel of the wooden mallet in my hands,

the bright balls moving toward wickets, the black
bread, the red wine, the girl in her blue suspension.

[FROM *Life Among Others*]

FISH

She is washed by white-water, white if she looked up.
She fingers the pebbles. This fancy of water for her,
touched now only by surf
and the brown temples of kelp.
There is a single boy in a caïque,
his drop line and the fish that moves off,
hooked, thinking itself free
with the taste of silver. The fish
is not destined to return with flesh of the hunt.
It moves for the woman on the beach without reason.
Its smooth body takes on the legs of the boy
in shallow water, grows a face
and stands in air, breathing
as if for the first time, and walks
to where the woman waits.
As the boy in the boat begins to sink
the fish touches the woman
on her hair that spreads upon her shoulders.
The kelp is green in the shallows beyond the breakers
where the boy descends—
the fish now tall in the light, the woman's hair, yellow
from the cliffs over her shoulders.
The boy descending. The woman looking up.
The fish bending to touch her.

CLAMS

The gift of clams is here, waiting
in the large bowl on the cutting table.
We are waiting: the clams
softly opening and closing.
I am in the kitchen, organizing
our hundred bottles of spice.
I take down oregano and sweet basil,
grate the cheese you forgot to cover,
and continue waiting.
The clams wait in their bowl.
They continue opening and closing—
closing when they think
I am looking at them. They are waiting
for the knife that will bare them to the world,
where they will taste the spices of the shelf,
giving up their grip on life.
I am waiting with this gift of clams.
In their opening and closing
they try to tell me something
of the hollow between their shells.
Or is it not to pry
into things I won't in the end understand?—
this gentle conversation in released sea air,
this gift of clams.

[FROM *Life Among Others*]

PHOTOGRAPH

I. D. H. *1921–1970*

I've never felt this way before, he said,
his last words, so the nurse said.
I went behind the curtain and touched his hand.
I thought of the drunk woman
who jumped into my car
as I waited for my parents
outside the restaurant the day we learned
of my father's illness. She lifted her dress
and said, *Want to feel something
you've never felt before?* I thought of my father
putting his arms around me, needing me
to carry him to the car.
I remember his pale eyes looking at me.
I took the last picture of him:
he stood in the driveway of our house
on Chandler Boulevard in a white T-shirt,
looking back at the camera. The smoke
of the cigar he held in his right hand
turned back against his thin wrist.
The curtain in the room was brown,
his hand, still warm, felt nothing.

WHITE TENT

I pitched a tent in an open field
near what you thought were white birds
searching for seeds in an open field.
They were white tents pitched
here and there, and inside each a fire
burned with a single voice.
I built myself out of these white tents:
it doesn't matter what each voice said,
that I was many things—a stick
beating a sad dog, a woman standing
in any empty house, looking away,
a young boy running in place on a beach.
In my tent I pieced something together
and went back out into the field,
clothed in these many voices. The tents
turned back to white birds. White birds
took flight, lifted off the ground
their ultimate kindness and watched me
grow smaller and smaller, a hornet
without wings, walking back to the road
where you waited, looking after the birds
as they lifted, and disappeared.

[FROM *Life Among Others*]

WHITE TRAIN

The night knows nothing of the chants of night
calling within it—songs that tremble
vibrato in blue air: Datura,
scent of your body that shakes itself from you
and becomes what the night never knows.
It is no dream that the white train shunts
within the chant of night.
The white voice of the muezzin, gentle
in its response, is no dream.
I know nothing more than scent,
the sense of touch where nothing sees.
I touch you
and it doesn't matter that the night
knows nothing.
Datura—white bell of the garden,
scent of the dead—does the muezzin
lie in his song? Is the white train
not going to return?
The night doesn't answer. It touches everything
and hears nothing. I touch you like this.
This is no dream. I know nothing.

WHITE CONTACT

There is a boy running along the beach.
But he is a boy only
if seen at a distance.
He is the man who left a house,
the woman who lived there,
and the white contact between them.
White, the color of clarity
where nothing has to live.
It matches everything and can go
anywhere. It fits in and is nothing.
White contact in a house where nothing
is said. Does he need to hurt her
in any other way? He cannot tell you.
She stands alone in the house
in the same way as when he was there.
It does not matter to her that he is gone,
or that he is running now toward something
far ahead that will remain small.
He rebukes her as he runs, he forgets her,
there is more and more to forget—
no contact, he thinks, only his feet
on the sand, smaller and smaller—leaving
behind the house, her hand—to become the boy,
running along the beach.

[FROM *Life Among Others*]

I AM A DANCER

There is no reason to be bothered,
to bother. Once you begin the anger
there is no telling where it will end.
But I sit down now and begin.
Is this the anger that takes up the stick?
The anger that is a silence in silence?
The thing not done, or done too late?
What a quiet little man I seem,
alone in a room with four walls
and, these days, something
of interest to make the days more interesting.
What is it the others want? Like?
They don't know. Do I miss them?
Let the dream take over now—white
train, white bird, white tent—white images
that lift away. This is how I work.
Myself, I am a dancer, feinting, refusing
to be there for you. It is not
that I don't care. The tent of dream
is a privacy, the bird a way out,
the train, power to keep on. I'm not
really unpleasant, and there is no crime
committed against others. Myself. No
madness, no crazy man behind bars. I
am the inmate. The crime
is only a little fear. I begin now
to beat it. To piece back together
the destruction of the walls.
I kick open the air and, my friend, I walk out.

[IV]

SEASONAL RIGHTS

WHITE FIELD

It is like standing beyond
a snowfield with a single
set of footprints across it
and you say, Those prints are mine
because no one else has ever been here.
All day the snow comes down,
all day you tell yourself what you feel,
but you remain in that place
beyond the snowfield.
Is there better proof
of your presence than
this open field, where you stand
now looking back across the white
expanse that is once more new to you?
As snow fills the places
where you must have walked,
you start back to where you began,
that place you again prepare to leave,
alone and warm, again intact, starting out.

THE CORPSE OF THE INSENSITIVE

The mountainside or pasture hills
are gauzy green and a few cows
sleep on the ground—a sign of rain
someone who doesn't know says. With tongues

the cows graze the body in the grass.

The woodsmoke from the house is soaked with **rain,**
the rain continues, low clouds,
wind, a chill and so on.
Yet we stand on the crossbeam redwood patio

and discuss the body in the grass.

It has been summer here and now it's fall.
No one is ready to begin the climb into winter.
Nothing in government has been settled
although a strike in Poland is over.
The moon spins in a socket, the young touch

through the filament clothes of the body in the grass.

End-of-the-season, turn-of-the-leaves,
so much left behind: summer pets, touch
and one or two small things said once
and never said again, or remembered

after addressing the body in the grass.

[FROM *Seasonal Rights*]

We rise in the first snow of winter
on the heat of woodfire,
our bodies partly spent in summer's slow decomposition.
We rise up on our own heat, simultaneous,

as if that body rising in the grass were ours.

OF THE AIR

Tonight, in the country, I stood awhile
under the dying oaks—the caterpillars
eat everything but stone—and one by one
starlings flung themselves at me
from the trees, pulling up
at the last moment and sweeping back
into the ornamentally fading sky.
At first I thought they were simply
playful, but they got closer and closer,
their whistling shrill.

If just one bird flew with intent into the window,
shattering the glass, I could believe
that there is something of substance
in their lives, but their bones are hollow—
I imagine that
without marrow they can't suffer,
that misery won't exist in air:
once torn from the earth
it is lifted up and dispersed.

It is still light out and I return
to prepare dinner. I have
something sorrowful keeping me here.

Somewhere there are people beginning
to make fires. Their lives,
of earthly marrow, work the fields.
At night, when the sun sets but it's still

[FROM *Seasonal Rights*]

early, women prepare small birds,
unstuffed, bony,
and the family eats.
And then it sleeps.
One of the young boys or girls
enters a weightless dream and rises,
not in the night, but through the air.

LATE

on lines by Elizabeth Bowen

It is late and the others have turned
off the lights to their rooms.
They are sleeping, or they are about to sleep,
or they are holding each other
in arms wrapped for sleep.
In the hotel only the lights of my room
call out to the solitary boats
staked to the warm bay.
What keeps me awake is indistinct.
You told me that without their indistinctness
things do not exist, you cannot desire them.
I think of you, what has not been said
and what remains unknown.
I return to claim what is unclear
as the guests of the hotel
finally release themselves to the night,
give the hotel over to its own settling in—
the natural progress of the night here.
I follow it. It becomes what is clear
as I hold both ends of dialogue,
asking my questions, answering for you.
If there were a truth in this hotel at night
it would bring me no sleep.
It makes nothing clear.
I say what comes to mind.
What comes to mind is the unsaid—
inflection your sweet device—your profile
at the window the day you turned to me to say
that those who never lie are never wholly alone.
It is late and the night air is fat with water.
I sit with you here, waiting for you to turn
again from that window and talk to me.

[FROM *Seasonal Rights*]

RETURN, STARTING OUT

There it is, the jagged sprawl of the familiar
landscape gripping the bay, urging itself
forward into the warming water of the Strait
and the lean winter fish that are picking up speed.

How much the same it is! Only I turned slightly, just now,
against it—this familiar! I touch it now and everything
is slightly less known and unknown—myself,
and others, houses the same color, repainted, or not here.

Now if I reach out into the air there is no sadness
in the empty space I receive, no sadness in the wood
of the oars when I take a rented boat into the bay
and let it drift, not driven but enchanted by current and wind.

Sitting in this boat, I look back at the rooms of houses.
What irritable knots of light they seem from here in half-light,
what irresistible nests of only a little warmth, smells
of whatever meats are over the braziers.

I am not fishing in this boat, it is becalmed.
I am not thinking deeply out here, no meditation.
I am floating, moving where the wood of the boat
moves, merely floating, looking back.

BIRTHRIGHT

I think they go back to visit
but not to remember,
they must have made some kind of peace
and let those years move on,
but if you let go too soon
some things disappear forever
and those who live there now
will inherit your past.

[FROM *Seasonal Rights*]

RETURN

Come back again and again, the fields no
longer hold their colors on limbs of light

over the earth, under the sky, over the soft
Dichondra, the clover and weeds that spread,

that pressed their dark root systems into these rich fields.
The old neighbors have passed quietly into the earth.

Your family has broken down and is traveling.
Still, this is where your mouth in humor first closed

over the mouth of the girl who lived behind you,
where you learned to live on the edge of talking.

Come back, the fields are gone and your friends are gone,
the girl behind you has married into another city, the roads

out of town are direct now and fast, and everyone
you knew is gone or no longer wants to know you.

But you must return, back to the long stretch of main street
reaching across the entire length of the valley,

back to the mild, midwinter days around Christmas,
back to what is now only remembered because nothing

is the same here anymore. There are no fields, nothing
edible on the land anymore—only the traffic moving

this way, then back again, then back again.
The light is no longer reflected in the earth

but you return because there is always something
that survives: come back again to old friends

living against dark fields, come back again, the family
holding dinner for you, come back, come back again.

[FROM *Seasonal Rights*]

NIGHT FOOD

I talked with those who fished the Santa Monica pier at three in the morning. They waited for crabs, for stray game fish, for bottom feeders. Some used flashlights, some rusty treble hooks to snag what was there. But none of them was a fisherman. Each one had, as I remember it, his or her own calling. There was the French philosopher who had fallen in love with Kierkegaard's Cordelia, and fished to remind himself of the depths of human emotions. There was the three-hundred-pound Mexican who brought one or two live bonito and set them out into the water with ninety-pound test and wire leader, hoping for the shark that came in each morning around five, or a stray black sea bass. There was also the black woman who fished from the darkest corner of the pier. She never talked, but always caught a gunnysack full of green crabs and was gone by four. Sometimes I took friends there, but they couldn't understand its particular appeal—the fish smell of the wood, the merry-go-round collapsed under white canvas, the live bait swimming in zinc pails—how strange it must have been to be there after a late movie and popcorn, to hear of Cordelia in the accent of the intense Frenchman in his blue turtleneck, or to watch the silent black woman pull green crabs out of the murky water. I took my friends for french fries at the all-night diner on the fishing deck and then home. Sometimes I returned to the pier, to resume conversation—perhaps with the bearded wino who maintained he had fished that pier ten hours a day for thirty-five years. He told me about the night the albacore and tuna swept in from deeper water and snapped the poles of everyone except the Frenchman, who was in the hospital having his gall bladder removed. I heard about the time the Mexican hooked a hundred-pound sea bass—with the help of the Frenchman and three tourists he managed to coax it into the net of a local Coast Guard cadet. What a gentle community we were, once the well-dressed couples left in their tuned-up repainted cars. For years I hardly missed a night. After work

in the hospital, I changed into a sweater and jeans, gathered my equip-
ment—for I had begun fishing after the second or third month—and
took the freeway to the pier. I doubt I caught more than ten fish
the entire time I spent there—I gave the hundreds of green crabs I
snagged to the black woman. What did it matter when I learned of
Cordelia, whom I too soon coveted? Or watched the tired Mexican
bring in tires, jungles of seaweed, and parts of outboard motors?
Maybe they are still there, all of them, their poles held resolutely in
the wet sea air, night fishing.

[FROM *Seasonal Rights*]

HOW TO EAT ALONE

While it's still light out
set the table for one:
a red linen tablecloth,
one white plate, a bowl
for the salad
and the proper silverware.
Take out a three-pound leg of lamb,
rub it with salt, pepper and cumin,
then push in two cloves
of garlic splinters.
Place it in a 325-degree oven
and set the timer for an hour.
Put freshly cut vegetables
into a pot with some herbs
and the crudest olive oil
you can find.
Heat on a low flame.
Clean the salad.
Be sure the dressing is made
with fresh dill, mustard
and the juice of hard lemons.
Open a bottle of good three-year old zinfandel
and let it breathe on the table.
Pour yourself a glass
of cold California chardonnay
and go to your study and read.
As the story unfolds
you will smell the lamb
and the vegetables.
This is the best part of the evening:

the food cooking, the armchair,
the book and bright flavor
of the chilled wine.
When the timer goes off
toss the salad
and prepare the vegetables
and the lamb. Bring them out
to the table. Light the candles
and pour the red wine
into your glass.
Before you begin to eat,
raise your glass in honor
of yourself.
The company is the best you'll ever have.

[FROM *Seasonal Rights*]

FOR CATS

They can take your breath away
but not from your mouth
directly. Old women
have passed this kind of thing
on—
there's almost no truth in it.

They can take your breath away
if you sleep with them sleeping
with their good fur over your mouth,
but this kind of thing happens almost
never—
cats won't stay long enough in that position.

They can take your breath away
when they are beautiful
and watchful with their affections,
if they know how to move and when
for you—
if they drop from great height without sound,

or clean themselves for hours in the sun,
or sit on your lap, their throats vibrato
against the thrumming of your fingers,
or stretch on their way out of the room, moving
perfectly—
they can take your breath away.

SNAPSHOT OF HUE

They are riding bicycles on the other side
of the Perfume River.

A few months ago the bridges were down
and there was no one on the streets.

There were the telling piles on corners,
debris that contained a little of everything.

There was nothing not under cover—
even the sky remained impenetrable

day after day. And if you were seen
on the riverbank you were knocked down.

It is clear today. The litter in the streets
has been swept away. It couldn't have been

that bad, one of us said, the river barely moving,
the bicycles barely moving, the sun posted above.

[FROM *Seasonal Rights*]

RIVER PASSAGE

The river town is too far now
by boat, for most,
and the forest has closed
over the only landing strip.

On the river nothing
beyond the outskirts
of the capital
makes a stranger welcome—

not even the inoculated
winter travelers so earnest
with sketch pads and pills,
ready for the darkness—

the darkness there is off
limits, the curfew begins
at sunset, is lifted
with the rising sun.

But we have come all this way,
it is the hot season along the river,
it is beginning for us.
We move through the overhang

of trees and river life, the razor
of water slicing into the dark vegetation
that one day opens onto the town
we've been awaiting for so long.

They come out to greet us as residents.
They come out to greet us as friends long lost.
They come out into the river light
to welcome us as one of their own,

and when we pass from river to land
we look again at the river
as it takes the first turn back
upriver to the capital of strangers.

[FROM *Seasonal Rights*]

DEAD FISH

The pale arc of line feeds
into the green of the bank
and drops its fly into the shallows
of the stream in shadow
without sound. The line floats down
onto water and the current
takes it on, deeper.
Cast after cast the fly moves
in the afternoon
from one edge of the stream
to the other, snapped into place
as I move downstream, replacing
cast with the imagined weight
of a feeder trout unseen in current.
Shadows wobble the stream.
I see a fish hung
near the bank, gills at rest,
life only in buoyancy,
its resistance against current.
I move close, drop the fly
upstream so it floats back
over the dull eyes of the sleeper
fish. The fly floats past.
It won't move. It won't move
as I move closer. It hangs there
and won't move as I bring down the rock
with terrified force. In the explosion
of water I see the white fungus
it has grown, the sucker mouth
and its full fish-body not trout.
It is imperfection I hate,

the age, the gamelessness of immobility,
the sudden decision to live.

When it floats to me
later, having fought to free itself
from branches of the stream trees,
I need its dead weight against my leg
to know ambition and its net, how it turns
on the object pursued,
dead now and my prize
as I cast in pale light,
the evening
pulled in on a fly.

[FROM *Seasonal Rights*]

TREES IN VARIOUS CLIMATES

There is something to say
in the company of others.
Alone, there is the viewing
of the evening sky, slate
and whitewash blue, the color
of the walls in the northern towns
of Morocco, although the sky
I'm thinking of is Italian
through stripped river trees
in the last days of the year.

In New Hampshire a few friends
tried to talk all afternoon one day,
about everything that was serious
and not serious in our lives.
We went from room to room trying,
and finally outside, into the thick
summer New England birch forest
which flushed the breath of ferns
at us, but all that came of it
was the attempt to talk, and that,
like many things unfinished,
became what was important.

Today, we each look out
at the weather in the morning,
the light of late afternoon,
and hold awhile that information.
The trees of Tangier, in December,
retain more color than the trees
of Rome, which let a light
into the room that reveals

too much of the secret sleep,
where everything is portrayed
as if actually uttered
through the skeletal trees.

[FROM *Seasonal Rights*]

NIGHT SCENE

The train passes through the night,
through tunnels like the night,
through open fields, at night.
The elemental racket of the rails
through the wine country of Umbria
keeps the two of us alert but saying nothing,
the wind whistling the second-class

compartments, our train from Rome to Terontola.
We see from the corridor windows
two circles of fire in a wine field,
perfect red arcs circumscribed in the night,
burning lightly without sound.
This is a sight we both know
will mean nothing in retelling,

that the literal fire of the two
circles in the middle of the night
will be only another event, attached to nothing.
I am relating this
far from the fact of the train ride.
The red of the flames might seem to us now
the color of local rubesco

or the deep red of Tuscan wines.
But this is something no longer important.
The train passed late in the night through
wine fields that held two perfect circles
of fire, and we two, friends and silent,
watched it pass and at the time said nothing.
It was enough.

THE ROMANCE

The Beginning

They met and in their meeting they were happy. She thought of others who had charmed her with delicacy and had left, and of the darkness in their hair. She thought such thoughts that sobered her, that brought her to him. And he in return thought of others before her, their gentle words and eyes that were as white coffins, containing roots that reached deeply to hold him. She believed that he, like her, believed that they held there in that moment of their meeting something unlike the white coffins that her eyes were for him. And in a similar way, he believed that his dark hair was without darkness for her. As they stood there with his fingers unsprung in hers and hers softly outside his, they believed that this was a meeting of two good things, that he would be there for her, and she, in return, would be there for him. And so in their meeting, with her hand and his hand for the first time one in the other, there was a happiness that both believed binding.

Status Quo

The birds with tiny particles of earth fly in through the eaves. It is autumn. It is the time of sunset. It is quiet. It is the country. It is a time for slowness of thought and movement. He tells her this, and she yawns. They know, both in their minor ways, a little secret: this then is the time of slowness. The birds and weather turn black and a winter night leans for them. There is a fire and he plays his favorite piece on their new piano. She talks. He smiles. He does not listen to her. The terrible lightness of Poulenc depresses him into brandy. She seems happy knowing he is happier than he has ever been. Her irritation is without irony. It is hours later that he, with too much brandy holding him, turns to her, a small glass of white wine from

[FROM *Seasonal Rights*]

the afternoon still in her hand, with a smile on his face. "The birds," she thinks. "The autumn," she thinks. She thinks, "The time of sunset, the time of slowness." When she removes his shirt it is her little secret that starts from his flesh. Terribly happy, he lays himself on top of her: the brandy. "Don't be catty," she whispers to him after he's fallen asleep.

Final Scene

"You're joking," he exclaimed. He felt immediate relief in this little burst of emotion, and yet saw that it made no impression upon her. She had been digging in her purse for the last few minutes, her arms buried in the rubbed-out leather pouch. "A child," he thought. Her hair suddenly fell into the purse alongside her arms. And she stopped for a moment and lifted from the purse a small dark pistol. He heard the hard sound of the bullet leaving the shell. He saw it stop to hang between them. She smiled as she rolled the black gloves up her long arms, and shoved her hair back over her shoulder. "Yes," he smiled. She stood and bent back down over him. Her tiny lips moved with care over his face. When she stood up for the final time, their eyes met.

PASSING

Sometimes you called on those
you'd never know
to come with you in place
of those you loved,
and talked to them
and touched them
and let them close purely
for sadness, for sadness
you'd hold them,
and you'd let them go.

[FROM *Seasonal Rights*]

ELEGIES FOR CARELESS LOVE

1. *Late October, Lake Champlain*

I've been trying to write you of that night
although you have no need
to be reminded of it—you haven't forgotten
the moon held on a stick of light
over the lake, its sudden appearance in our bed
on my shoulder, on your shoulder.
We can let it pass but nothing is over
and the imprint of your feet and hands
remains in my hands. I remember now
the moon, the lake and the room
of Vermont pine—the space
of those days when all it could do
outside was rain. Forget those nights,
that place, when we were at ease
with our predilection for the removed
nagging us back
to sleep and your dream of a blue bottle
filled with an unknown scented fluid.
Now I give you a blue container—
scent-filled—with slices of paper notes,
those phrases that can't be said.

2. *Woodsmoke, Vermont*

The woodsmoke drifted into the car
every time we passed a house
on that road down the center of Vermont,
and each time you told me how you loved
woodsmoke. The weather was rain

and that week was like living
in the already past—everything part
of some other time:
the odor of the room in that town,
the women on Geritol who sat
all day in the lobby.

                              And all night the scent
of woodsmoke drifted to us
in our wooden bed, all night the rain
fingered the wooden shingles
above our room. What could we have said?
Below us the old women were held
in woolen blankets
and the soft white sheets of the inn.
And there we were, holding on
to each other,
already in the process of letting go.

3. Sleeper

I held you in the front room.
When we woke the fire was nearly out
and the wine had almost
worn off.

You said you couldn't sleep
being held,
yet you slept.

I asked if we should go
into the other room,
but you said no, that you
could never go there,
that it would be the end of everything.
We went into the other room

and it was the end of nothing,
or not of anything that had started.

I think about what you said that night.
Nothing had started that wasn't always there.

You never slept before the fire,
you never went half in dream
to the other room,

and you only dreamed
that as I held you there
you slept.

4. *Your Hands*

You've probably put on
your white sweater

and plaid skirt,
your boots and now

shake down your hair
as you enter some dining room

vague and vain and a little
lonesome for our dark

late-night dinners in the city
when you were happy with

the candlelight, the single rose,
the hand closing on yours.

Isn't it always like that for a while?
Everything stopped, held there

with only the hands in motion.
Yours must be so cold—

do they deflect snow?—
I took them in mine,

your hands that had given up
their warmth for so long.

5. No Letters

My friend, how sad you were here—
but not too sad, not enough
in league with happiness to be happy.

The house in the Midwest, is it cheerful?
In your chair with your afternoon drink
remember how you went

this way and that way, wanted
one thing
and wanted another.

The sun sets there
but continues west. Look after it.
Listen closely as the low song begins:

from the huts of the poor,
from the tract homes of the poor,
from the mansions of the poor,

oh careless love.

[FROM *Seasonal Rights*]

6. *An End*

Occasionally, it was only night. I mean
you didn't come back again

and in the morning there was nothing
left unless you had carelessly left

your scent in the room.
I remember nothing more than the idea of scent.

The only thing to do in the morning
was to begin again without you,

which I have begun to do.
The nights are shorter and spring

has come, and another who takes more care
with what she cares about

than you. I will miss you.
Do not expect applause.

NUDE

In one of Watteau's pencil sketches
there's a woman sleeping on her side,
partly covered, the space behind her
darkly penciled in, her right arm
reaching out, probably around someone
who has left.
What makes me think her arm
is not merely cast out
is the way Watteau sketched dampness into her hair,
the way he remembered to pencil in
the good-time cloth-bracelet on that wrist,
and the space next to her,
which he left without a mark.

[FROM *Seasonal Rights*]

THE STORM

The Italian police stopped us today
as I passed a tiny Fiat on the road
from Perugia to Umbertide.

They were behind a few cypress trees
and I couldn't see them in my hurry
to beat home the storm over Firenze.

They told me I'd passed over an unbroken line,
although, standing there, I did find a small space
near where we stood and tried to make my case,

but we all smiled—the Italian workmen
had run out of paint that day, it was their mistake
although I would have passed anyway

and the two thousand lire it cost me
can't buy decent pasta anymore. The air
was stopped and it darkened over Tuscany.

We drove on into the storm and beat it home
as I knew we would, past the guinea fowl
and geese in our village of Polgeto,

and soon the rain began to fall, large drops
at first raising the dust, then gluing it down,
then filling the water tanks of Umbria.

The peasants sitting outside Polgeto's shops
stopped talking awhile, and the tree insects
too stopped their chirrs, as if to acknowledge

the storm. And then they started up again.
I awaited this beginning—nothing
is plain when heard again after silence.

I wanted to say more, how a storm registers
on the stony faces of the men outside
the *alimentari*, the insects' shutdown.

What will survive, remembering all this,
is something else—not the police or the rain
or the skies building up over the north,

but how out of the daily incidents
we find the distance not too long to go,
that we can go that distance, and continue on.

[FROM *Seasonal Rights*]

THE LAST DAYS OF THE YEAR

Sometimes the days must
  fly by
    as they say,

one year palms
  inhabited by wind and rain,
    the wet smell of wool

in the Berber markets,
  the next our room
    on Isola Tiberina

off the little Piazza
  San Bartolomeo, river-damp
    with the river patrol

at the point, waiting
  to drag out the suicides
    and driftwood.

Above Italy
  the skyline is cypress,
    black imago pressed

against the pale mauve
  of Roman winter sunset.
    You're out looking

for something in the shops
  off the Corso and I'm sitting over
    the Tiber, remembering that

one night last year
  I went deep into the markets
    of Marrakesh to find

the little birds
  made from the green
    malachite of the Atlas.

You must have sat like this
  over your mint tea thinking
    about other years

at home, your mother
  and her mother baking together
    and cleaning the silver

with the special paste
  that is one of the
    remembered decorations;

you must have thought
  I'd been gone a long time,
    waiting as it got later,

as I wait now
  for you, the same sounds
    of the cars outside, passing by.

[FROM *Seasonal Rights*]

SPEND

Diminishing returns she said,
you've got to make up your mind someday—
good money after bad my father would have added
had he thought about it, and he did.
He didn't talk much period, his pursuits
being bargains, discounts, the model
that looked like the real thing but never was.
I told my friends he worked in the metal business—
they thought I said *meadow* business,
but asked no questions and I didn't correct them.
He died too early to understand someone else
and I grew up too slowly to help him out.
After these ten years it doesn't matter anymore
because I can understand it all. What comes back
is not what you've given, that much we know
no matter how slowly we've grown into the world.

But you have to decide someday, this way or that,
to toss the good after the bad or whatever it is
you have to give. I have the usual memories,
the collective sadness of growing up among the dying,
never knowing to say enough at the right time—
I am my father's son, but I've learned to spend
with a carelessness that would have won me nothing
in my father's eyes, they were so pale blue.
Living well doesn't cost much if style
is what you're after. My friends can all have
the best of what they want, but their wants
are simple and elegant. My father wanted so little

that it cost him everything, with nothing coming back.
But he would have said that if you wait long enough
something will come back. Diminishing returns.
Nothing that needs to come back comes back.

PORTONCINI DEI MORTI

In the *Analects* Confucius says,
The way out is via the door. How is it
that nobody recognizes this method?

In Gubbio, an Umbrian city
the most purely medieval in Italy, the buildings
have what the Italians call *portoncini dei morti*,
the little doorways of the dead.
When the dead of the family went through the door
for the last time they plastered it up.

It wasn't for the dead they did this,
but for themselves—they knew
death was the last farewell,
plastered or not, remembered or not.

Confucius was wrong, wasn't he? A door
is not the simplest solution.
I'm thinking about history and the departure
of the loved, about fathers
or men who raised sons they couldn't know.

I'm talking to those who have no ghost doorway
to mark their leaving us, who were carried
to the place that takes care of lost love—
in our country people die away from home,
it's part of the economy,
and the economy of loving.

The medieval Italians knew something
about dying and about love,
they closed the door for the dead.

What do the dead open for us
but the door that opens onto what there was?
What do we do for the dead but lower them
into the earth, shovel earth over
their eyes, and this, like the plaster
of the Italians, keeps the living out of
the way of those dead we have lost.

Intelligence is not needed to find a door
after death in the presence of love,
nor are doors answers to anything
that hides some part of ourselves.
The question is how to turn back—
the Italians were right: let the dead
leave us unattended and unencumbered.
Let us build new doors that the family
may leave together. This is the solution
and Confucius too was right,
that we will find new ways of being together
among the living.

[FROM *Seasonal Rights*]

[V]

TANGO

VISITORS

At low tide, midsummer, I walked out to the mussel beds
at tide's edge. Still wet, the blue-black shells,
trussed together with hairlike bonds, waited
for the tide to move back in. I don't walk here
at low tide—it's a landscape too recently lived in
and therefore unpredictable. But I was collecting mussels

for dinner because the markets were closed
and guests from the city expected something from the sea.
I would steam the mussels in a little vermouth and toss them
with fresh basil from the back yard and a pound of pasta.
I pulled up two or three beds and placed the clenched mollusks
in the zinc pail I brought, and as it was still early,

and mild, I walked up the beach, chiding myself for not doing so
more often. A small mist like those on Guam in the war movies
of the fifties began to roll in behind the tide.
Farther on, there was a woman in a bathing suit asleep
on her towel. I continued along, walking over the sharp,
encrusted rocks of low tide for a mile, and then started back.

The air turned cool as the wind and tide pursued the evening
in an unpleasant way. When I passed, the woman
was as I'd left her nearly an hour earlier. Her head faced away
from me, back toward the line of houses,
but I guessed she was young—her hair, the shape of her body
and its posture in sleep—still there in the cooling afternoon,

the sun about to drop through the horizon.
I stopped, hoping she would hear me and turn, surprised
out of afternoon sleep, slip on her shift, and run off to her house.
I stood awhile and then spoke to her, first softly, then louder.

Then I leaned down and touched her. She was cool, almost cold,
and very smooth. She turned to me, suddenly awake and angry.

I said I lived next door . . . she hadn't moved for so long,
the temperature going down, the tide and dinner hour approaching.
She had difficulty understanding my right to this concern.
It must have been the pail of mussels that kept her from screaming.
When she looked at it I told her I was collecting for dinner,
that I wouldn't have bothered her, it was neighborly concern,

what we're accused of not acting on in moments of trouble.
She dressed, thanked me with suspicion still afloat, and moved
off the beach. In my kitchen I found a large pot to steam open
the mussels—their shells turned darker in the electrical light
and opened for good. The guests from the city arrived
and over pasta, which they cheered, we discussed the latest

felonies reported in the city papers. I wondered
what the young woman said to those who shared her dinner.
Perhaps she told them that as she slept in the afternoon sun
the man next door knelt beside her and touched her awake,
wanted to know if she was okay as he held a zinc pail
of collected mussels. After our meal, after my friends

had retired for the night with their guest towels
and fresh linen, I walked out to the water, which was set
with a single white plate, and wandered awhile down the beach.
I imagined touching that cool flesh with no response coming back,
turning her over to discover the damage all at once, startled
not out of sleep but out of the languorous, cooling afternoon.

This is the meager distance I've allowed the dying to come,
I thought, that moment after I touched her, before she turned
her girlish face to me in accusation, as I balanced beside her
with a pail of mussels, waiting for her.

[FROM *Tango*]

TANGO

I'm your private dancer,
a dancer for money . . .
　　　　—FROM A TINA TURNER SONG

When Celina arrived the floor was on fire.
You could tell by her hips and her mouth
she was built for the tango.

Glasses of clear amber danced the tables
on the tango rhythm. You could tell
this place was built for the tango.

The room on its axis turned, and turned the dancers
around the room
hung with the haze of tango,

the haze of cigarette smoke and the smoke
of braziered meats, the smoke of bodies—
you could tell by their hips and their mouths

they were built for the tango, the smoke
from their bodies locked onto the tango beat,
the colored lights, the white and black

dancers turning on their notes, and you could tell
they were built for the tango.
When Celina danced she danced in dance-hall heaven,

and everyone knew she was built for the tango—
you could tell by her hips and her mouth.
When she arrived the place was already on fire.

Anita Lozano sang the tangos that night and every other.
You could tell by her mouth she was built
for tango, bearing in on the lyrics, letting them go.

The couples, by this hour built for the tango,
rose up in the heat on the sweat and sweet scent of anise,
on the voice of Anita Lozano that *was* tango—

you could tell by her mouth.
You could see how their hips followed her tango soul,
her tango lyrics. Celina took the rhythm from Anita Lozano

because she was the queen of tango,
because she was built for the tango. You could tell
by her hips and her mouth she was built for the tango.

[FROM *Tango*]

BAR ESCARGOT: A STORY

Moe served drinks in the Bar Escargot, a youthful Liberian saved by Peter, the English owner, from a cannibalistic sect of the Masons.

I would find my way there after *tapas* at the Spanish bars above the port, after the European *paseo* along the rue de Pasteur.

The Escargot was dark, empowered with the scent of West Africa, vague felony, and some piece by Beethoven from Peter's complete works on the tape deck any hour of the day.

When I arrived, Moe was often beating a dust mouse behind one of the couches of the room, and when he saw me he set down the broom, straightened a piece of colonial furniture from the previous century, put on his white waiter's coat, and served me a beer called Stork, the national bird of Morocco.

Then he brought out the chessboard, and he and I would sit down to play before the other customers arrived from their solitary dinners.

Moe didn't talk much beyond his speaking vocabulary of twenty or thirty words, but understood everything in English, French, German, and Moghrebi.

It never took him longer than five minutes to complete a game against me, although I had won tournaments in the parks of Los Angeles.

Moe had a huge Alsatian called Parrot, trained by Peter to attack the natives; the rest of us moved without harm, casually through the bar, talking to Moe and Peter without tension.

As the night wore on the regulars began to appear at their appointed hours.

They were all solitaries, cast out from one place or another, their histories never referred to or grand fictions of the present.

They were mostly beyond seventy, living in rented rooms off the boulevard, wearing loud clothes—the males in reverse makeup, the females blurring facial lines with unsteady hands.

They met at the Escargot each night and ran through their trumped-up agendas over strange mixed drinks Peter knew—as he knew each of them, their names, the hour of their arrival, the hour they would take their leave.

Among this clientele, Moe moved like a sullen predator, laughing suddenly at nothing and continuing on, preying on empty glasses.

And Parrot, kicked from one sleeping spot to another, kept an eye on the door, an eye on the ever-moving Moe.

One evening around Christmas Moe was taken to Beni Makada, the local house of mental detention, the state hospital, after he was caught chasing one of the regulars up the rue de Fez with Peter's meat cleaver.
A few months later he returned, but the currents that had run through him like medication had turned him into something different.
He was no longer engaged by the dust that roamed the floors of the Escargot.
And he lost now at chess, which I think broke what was left of his heart.

After that he and Parrot stayed in the kitchen and Peter cleared the tables as he served his drinks to the regulars, who diminished as the new year started out, deserting the Bar Escargot for the Ranch Bar, its upbeat chili and Country Western music.
That summer Peter died of a blood disease and the Bar Escargot was turned over to the King.
No one knew where Moe and Parrot were, they disappeared after Peter's death, although it was rumored he had returned to Liberia aboard some freighter he caught in one of the southern ports.
After I returned to the States I heard from a friend that a spree of killings had taken place in the Dradeb, an outlying residential district, and Moe had been discovered in the area and returned to Beni Makada for life.

The Bar Escargot, Peter, Moe, and Parrot weren't anything the long-time residents of Tangier would remember, or wish to remember—a low-class bar that might have served a Greyhound station had it been in Des Moines.
But I began to wonder about Moe in Beni Makada and years later finally went to see him—it took weeks in green and yellow offices to get a visitor's pass.
I arrived one morning in late spring when the entire compound was enclosed in fog and the sounds that emerged from that indistinct structure were not something you wanted to take away with you.
I was led through a series of gates and courtyards, keys and locks and sullen guards who had been there too long.
In one of the inner courtyards a low, whitewashed door opened and a middle-aged Moe sprang out on all fours.

[FROM *Tango*]

The light blinded him, as if it had been his first in the ten years he'd been there, and he remained stationary, confused by his sudden release and the strange voices filling the courtyard.
And then he lifted one hand to his eyes and tried to bring me back from some dark corner of his life.

From the dirt of the courtyard, he looked up at me.
His head was shaved and he wore the remains of something that looked like long underwear.
He looked up at me and laughed the laugh I remembered from the Bar Escargot. I remembered the scent of Africa rising on the clinking glasses, the ever-attentive Parrot, and the last disturbing string quartets Peter had committed to tape.
And then he grabbed my leg.
Before the guards could move he opened his mouth as if to bite me, but instead called out into the textured air of the damp courtyard, *Parrot! Parrot!*—and then the guards had him, applying to his hard body their guards' sticks, pulling his hands behind his back and pushing his forehead into the dirt of the thickening courtyard.
And when they dragged him back to his cell, or whatever lay behind that low doorway, I saw women emerge from a room in the back of the building with small metal foil-covered trays, which they pushed into the openings cut at the base of the doorways.
They placed the trays halfway through, so the hinged doors rested on the food being offered.
I suppose they wanted to know who was eating without having to open the door onto whatever was alive in there.
When I left it seemed that as the locked gates clicked open for me the trays, in unison, were pulled through the shuttered openings into the waiting darkness.

SEÑOR EXCELLENT

I was taken there as a child,
the old Farmer's Market on Fairfax.

Spectacular displays of fruit blossomed
everywhere you looked, and men in white

behind glass made candy, their giant vats
of chocolate bubbling like the La Brea Tar Pits.

And there was always something to eat
whichever way you turned.

But the important event at Farmer's Market
was the stop in front of Señor Excellent.

He had a vocabulary limited to one shrill catcall,
a few opening bars of a song, and a number of *hellos*

varying in pitch and intensity. What I remember **now**
is not what Señor Excellent said, but the wisdom

and irony in the eyes of that myna bird.
We stood around whistling and clicking

and one of us would inevitably try out a few **words**
of endearment. Have you ever listened carefully

to what people say to talking birds
when they think they are alone? Señor Excellent

just looked at us, his expression one of agony
and disgust. I can picture him

[FROM *Tango*]

resting on his mauled stick, calmly breathing
and watching us—picking at something

under his wing, going down for a seed, lifting
himself back up with his candy-corn beak—

and I know that his was a life not so different,
witnessing the utterances of the human race.

THE HOBBYIST

In late August she decided to make Thanksgiving turkeys
   out of crepe paper to sell the merchants of the Valley.
      I remember rolls of it around the house that fall,

browns and tans for the body, the unlikely objects she used
   for the head—the beak and wattle, those deadpan eyes
      that should have been balls of amber.

Every year it was something different. When I was eight
   she painted old sewing boxes, calling back
      into action her set of twenty-year-old oils. The box

she kept for herself, its deep green-blue, the dusky rose
   flowers and their green-black leaves, three to a side,
      now holds that darkness I have come through.

One spring she sold refinished tables inlaid with mosaics
   I bought with her at the local hobby center. There was no end
      to the colors to choose from—bright reds and yellows,

plain whites opaque and transparent, royal purple
   and forest green, deep agatelike admixtures of colors
      that changed as you turned them under the neon lights

of the store—and the white powder that held those blocks
   of color: *grout*, the name of something
      gnarled and old, more suited to the clamps

that cut the tiles. She practiced on plywood boards
   before setting the tiles into the tables and fixing them
      forever, everything set out by number

[FROM *Tango*]

once the pattern emerged. I have one of the practice boards
    whose tiles never found their way into a table.
        She set the tiles with glue, grouted them in,

and gave the board to me for my first departure.
    The colors: cobalt blue and black, dusky rose,
        and her inevitable green-blue. I use it as a platter

that carries on the surface its own history
    of those years when objects are what *can* remain neutral,
        can attach themselves to the ongoing memory

and become part of the lasting fabric of what can be recalled.
    And later on, when it becomes impossible to participate
        in such simple ways, you begin a project for yourself,

to pursue what you imagine you've a gift for—talking,
    moving from place to place, keeping yourself out
        of harm's way. It was something domestic I received,

handed down from that early art—turkey and table,
    the painted sewing box that held her mending,
        the needles and thimbles, the hundred threads.

AN EARLY DEATH

It is the first death that seems so open
  to revision, as if later on,
    at some ordinary hour, the dead
      will again be with us wherever we are.

It was a Catholic funeral for the boy
  who came home one day, went to sleep
    in the lasting light of early summer,
      and didn't wake up for the evening meal.

During the service I watched his mother,
  who was Spanish, as the event burned
    dimly in her, the off-red of roses
      almost dry, a small pulsing emanation,

not light exactly but something just barely
  aglow. They couldn't agree on the cause
    of death, but for me he was just gone,
      first one day and then all the others.

It occurs to me these many years later
  that the funeral provided me
    an introduction, and then the possibility
      of resuming my own life, although

I often thought I saw my friend trimming
  the ivy in front of his house on Chandler
    during the endless summer afternoons
      of the San Fernando Valley,

[FROM *Tango*]

the silver cross he wore filmed with dirt
    kicked up by the trimmer. By autumn
        I was able to let him go.
            He no longer appeared on our street

in his white parochial-school shirts.
    Sometimes, when I sat with his mother
        while she prepared her survivor's meal
            and we talked in a casual way

of her son, I studied the large reproduction
    of Velázquez's *Surrender of Breda*
        that hung on a wall near the kitchen
            where we sat. I counted the horses

and soldiers as they stood in a line,
    their spears held upright, catching a diminished
        amber light, posing as if for Velázquez
            himself, impatient to remove their armor

and return to the tables of Rioja
    and heavy bread. It is the quality
        of light in that painting that brings back
            my friend's Spanish mother, the vermilion

smoldering like old fire behind
    the horsemen, under the unilluminated
        green shake of the deciduous trees
            Velázquez chose to leave out of the painting.

She talked quietly about her son
    as she prepared her meals. Her sorrow
        was alive, unrelinquished, without
            revision. She often tried to explain

how he cared for me, our friendship;
  the vocabulary was hers, her meaning
    embarrassing information at that age.
      She allowed me to return

something of her son, although this certainly
  didn't occur to me then, and perhaps
    not for many years.
      It is afternoon on the East Coast—

when I think of my friend
  it is she who is there, who takes his place.
    We have both lived out that early death,
      and we have this far survived the austere light

that fixes those men in *Surrender*
  of Breda, each of them waiting around
    under the protection of Velázquez's
      invisible trees, in the little light left them.

[FROM *Tango*]

SUMMER NIGHTS

for my mother

You took me to see your friend, a youngish man
    who lived encased in iron and spoke
through a machine that made his voice
    sound underwater, his head propped
in such a way that I imagined it was
    unattached to what there was of his body.

In the summer of 1952 I lay awake
    in the hot, endless nights
with cars drifting listlessly
    down Chandler Boulevard, their lights
sliding the walls of my room and moving off
    into the desperately calm summer air.

On those nights I thought of your childhood,
    how the doctors wrapped your poor legs
with wool and tar, your mother bathing you
    through the plagued Chicago summer—
the smell of wet wool still makes you sick.

    In the night, as I awaited the morning
that could find my thin body motionless and locked,
    I listened with sentimental care
to my sister crying softly to herself
    in dream, you and our father talking
in a muffled way in your bedroom,
    the low, barely discernible static
of his transistor radio.

It was as if in those airless rooms
there was no hope of surviving the night,
    that everything was endless and dark,
with sleep coming only with the lights
    of cars, the final victory of their lulling
sure movement, drifting steadily awhile
    on the walls of my room, and passing on.

[FROM *Tango*]

HEAVENLY ORNAMENTS

The frame of human happiness is time.
—DEREK WALCOTT

They are, so many of them, too far away now
to recall.
Outside the moon rises and slowly

the anemic globe fills with light during a cycle of nights,
blossoming full over the ragged beaches of Maine
where those friends who remain close

lie down to sleep.
Over the Pacific rim of Los Angeles
my sisters in their new lives with others

lie down to sleep.
Over the steelworks
studding the three rivers of Pittsburgh

my mother lies down to sleep.
Where I am, the tallest oak in the back yard
clutches at the rotating night-light

as it rolls through the named figures
of constellations.
I look into the night sky,

above the pine, above the wild apple,
the larch and rock maple,
and see the determined configurations of stars

in place at their appointed hours.
And for those too far away,
or too close—we look *for* you

as we lay our tired, mortal selves to bed
with all the constellations shining. Understand,
the heavenly ornaments burn only for the living.

[FROM *Tango*]

SCARS

They are the short stories of the flesh,
can evoke the entire event
in a moment—the action, the scent
and sound—place you there a second time.

It's as if the flesh decides to hold
onto what threatens its well-being.
They become part of the map marking
the pain we've had to endure.

If only the heart were so ruthless,
willing to document what it lived
by branding even those sensitive
tissues so information might flow back.

It's easy to recall what doesn't heal,
more difficult to call back what leaves
no mark, what depends on memory
to bring forward what's been gone so long.

The heart's too gentle. It won't hold
before us what we may still need to see.

CALL

The sharp, insomniac cry of a seabird
calls me from a complicated sleep.

Outside, the even slap of bay surf
on the stones of the beach below the window.

It should be possible to turn again
on the spit of sleep and reenter what's left

of the night. But I climb down a staircase
carpeted in fifties green and go through the back door

where the dead-white moon waits bloated above the summer
boats, set in the glassy glaze of the bay's brittle.

As a child the night sometimes played the riddle-of-no-waking,
and my attempt to imagine the day I wouldn't wake

kept me awake and uneasy for the duration of the night.
It seemed that in the end we just *do* wake, regardless.

On such a night I lay struggling with the car lights
passing down Chandler Boulevard when I heard a car door

slammed hard, then the hollow clacking of a woman's
heels down Chandler toward the Tierneys' house.

The car started up fast, came to a stop
again, and I heard raised voices in the cricket-timed dark,

followed by a woman screaming through her own echo. Then
no sound. When her voice returned on the wakeful nights that followed,

[FROM *Tango*]

I sometimes tried to imagine a woman so lonely and alone
that she volunteered for the late, difficult hours,

pursued by those who torment women in the night
from cars. Sometimes I saw my sister struggling

to free herself from what I heard that night,
to reach the best citizen of our quiet neighborhood.

Sometimes the woman became the women I slept with
as I grew through a tardy adolescence, their graceful bodies

seemed to me, as they lay in my poorly furnished rented rooms,
so frail that if they called out from their own troubled sleep

I would be there to reach through the dark to hold them
above whatever opaque waters might be rising inside them.

I hear her voice on many nights I wake from sleep alone—
like this night, coming out of sleep, not knowing

where, at first, as I put the room together.
Tonight the gulls must sleep wherever they find shelter,

although one is in the air, throwing its piercing alarm
along the coast, where I stand holding what memory has brought along,

the shrill voice wounded by fear that carries now on the cries
of the unmolested feeding birds at sunrise, just rising.

PARTING WORDS

It's a small town somewhere
away from any serious body of water.
The sky has picked up the available dust
and the sun poaches itself
on one of the horizons.
This is where you meet, a café?
Call it the Café of Four Flowers,
where they serve chilled beer
and leave you alone
with the music one of you selected
coming in. It's dark
and the lights are colored,
the right color for what you have to say.
What was it that seemed so available
driving into this town,
that vanished when you saw her white car
in front of the café,
her pale arm in its white holster
wedged out the window, waiting
because you were late again?
Always late, isn't that right?
She thinks it means something,
right? This time it means
you don't want to be here,
a town you might have come to
before the age of attachment.
The waitress is the same woman
who serves you all over the country,
only the length of her skirt
and the color of her hair change.
She'll toss your change down
and pick it up without a smile.

[FROM *Tango*]

Who's her lover?
Who serves her the afternoon beer?
It's this kind of thinking that keeps your mind
on subjects other than leaving,
which is why destiny has brought you here:
to make it clear why you're going
and what it means.
But she's not talking.
She's doing what she's been told
is right, she's waiting
for you to say something.
You wonder what this will mean
a year from now and already you have the answer:
it won't mean anything
because she will have forgotten all about you,
your address, the number of your phone,
and the Café of Four Flowers.
She'll be with someone
who speaks even less than you
and resigned to it.
And where will you be?
You'll be right where you are today,
in some café
with your car cooling down
in the damned parking lot.
You'll be there with nothing to say,
ready to pay the bill,
hand over a little change
to the same woman,
although she'll have dyed her hair,
and fashion will have lifted her skirt a little.

SUMMER STORM

All day the storm's
tried squeezing out the light,
a huge mist grows,

and the wind comes up—
nothing to take the boards off
the house, but enough

to set us all on edge,
although these winds,
unlike the easterly winds

of the Mediterranean,
carry nothing but air.
Only a few gulls

climb the wind and swing
over the house—
the diving birds gone,

the herons that feed
at the water's edge gone,
and the ducks are sheltering

somewhere out of the storm.
I have the fire started,
a little broth on the stove,

and the house is closed
to the storm—
only its light

[FROM *Tango*]

can reach us.
It picks out the white boats
in the bay and fires them

with a luminist's white,
igniting everything white,
and, as suddenly,

as the mist changes density,
is defused. The light enters
the afternoon and finds us

at work like this:
one is asleep
in an upstairs room,

another reads in the runway
where the view is only forest,
the more stable landscape

in a storm. She's reading
a story about injustice
and the right to extremes,

of something uncomplicated
like a pair of horses starved
by angry men, the death of the hero,

and the darkening the author sensed
in 19th-century Europe.
So she's reading on a cane couch,

her friend is preparing the evening meal,
and I'm on my way out of the house
to walk awhile in the afternoon,

or what's left of it.
We've lost something here:
a day of perfect light,

a little time in the sun
with the birds
at work, carrying out

their natural chores,
the flock of sails adrift
at another end of the bay.

But I'm not thinking of sunlight,
or the sailing boats,
or the horses of Michael Kohlhaas.

I could lie down
with my sleeping friend
and hold her as the storm

terrorizes the landscape,
sleep awhile next to her
and wake in the night

with the sound of rain
barely audible, tapping
the walls of the house.

I remain outside
in the rain and the darkening
and look back at the house

where those close to me
are at work,
whatever it is.

[FROM *Tango*]

The white, heavy column
of smoke rises
into the mist, and below,

at the smoke base, the fire
gives to them its necessary heat.
I'll stay here a little longer

and return after dark, to share
the evening meal, the fire,
the small-talk, our right to all this.

TO A FRIEND
SHOT ON A MEXICAN BUS

He's one of the hard talkers,
hitchhiker, runner,
cold-water swimmer.
He walks Broadway
after the bars have closed,
whistling at those willing
to commit harm,
can ignore the tremendous
rush of leftover fish
in the street-trash
of oriental restaurants.
He has fought the wars
he could have
and writes letters of length
that break down upon themselves.
If we talk about him
over a few drinks
we remember the cadence
of his walk,
the arguments he had
with each of us.
He's the one who lost an eye
looking for the club of a pre-bop jazzman
in a forties Kansas City
back street off Troost Avenue,
the friend who called at no-man's hour
to say he needed a friendly voice.
He's the man on the Mexican bus
shot for insulting the dust.
Where were the women

[FROM *Tango*]

to take him in at night,
the family—
where are we,
the days so entangled these many years
later?
Haven't we
understood this far?
We've hung back,
which was the right thing to do.
We won't insult the dust and die,
we won't die
during the moments
we believe ourselves
beyond the cycles of nature.
We won't die insulting the dust.

PREPARATIONS FOR
THE END OF THE EVENING

The light is Spanish on the Moroccan back streets,
late winter, the air begins to hold a little
of the lemon vegetation, the sound of dogs
and flutes carries up the valley, late afternoon.

It is cold enough to continue burning wood
and stay inside. Above, the clouds
promise an early evening, inflated on light,
full, but not ready to come the distance forward.

Although uninvited, I know they have begun
the preparations for the evening meal upstairs;
their cooking finds its way here to remind me
of my own meal, still uncut on the counter.

The watered plants use up the day's fluid
and darken on the terrace; the caged birds there
have shut down for the night, the pets
of a boy here. These nights can be spent

in the custodial care of the fire, the out-of-print
novel, and a little pacing between front door
and back window, where I watch the streetlamps
snap on, listen to the frogs starting up

in the riverbed, where they say a beautiful woman lives
to seduce unwary men. She has the feet of a goat
and those who look into her eyes go crazy—
this being part of the local mythology. Late winter,

[FROM *Tango*]

and blowing from the east the *levante*,
a wind that pursues the restless population.
The palms appear to change color at night in this season;
the visual rearrangements in the street alarm those

foreign to this place. Who *is* waiting for you there?
Under the streetlamps the little stages
await their players. The sound of dishes upstairs,
the house lights of the valley going out,

the metal shutters slamming shut—
preparations for the end of the evening.
The fire here will always need another stick of wood,
the pot another cut of meat, another sliced vegetable.

The light from the fire plays on the neutral.
At this hour there is no sound that can be identified,
there is nothing in the river except stones and sand
over which the opaque water continues.

THE LESSON

Where have they gone?
she asked her father.

To the orchards,
he replied,
where the apples hang
until they can't wait
any longer.

To the shade trees in town,
he said,
where the citizens are distracted
from their daily work
by the musical, repetitious
pill-will-willet
and rapidly repeated
kip-kip-kip
before the tree birds take flight.

To the large scattered trees
where only space abides
and the blown current
of air in open places.

The child is on a softening redwood
watching her father,
listening to the *thwack* of his ax
against the heartwood,
the furred vibration
of the cat's throat in her lap
and the good muted thudding
again and again at her breast.

[FROM *Tango*]

THE DEATH OF LI PO

*It is reported that the poet Li Po fell out of a boat
and was drowned when he tried to embrace the
moon's reflection on the water.*

Not even their master calligraphers
had a configuration for gesture
that deep, no combination of a master's strokes
could have anticipated his disappearance,
it wasn't in the language.

The hour he pushed away from the shore is uncertain—
his boat light, riding high in the water
and colored indecorously,
nearly celebratory in its pursuit of restraint.

The dark, irregular pattern of current
on the water took him out
to one of the windless centers of the river.

The boat, stilled, turned
on the unseen guiding current
under the pure intensity of moon.

He motioned through his fingers,
beyond now the swirling eddies,
the paired butterflies and various mosses.

He removed his colorless robe
that had nothing of the impure to violate
the water's white abstraction.

The moonlight that was everywhere
reflected around the circumference of his arms,
which he spread to embrace the white surrogate
imprinted thinly on the skin of water
as he passed through that perfect circle of light.

AT DANTE'S TOMB

Too austere even for Dante

this place of interment
   at seaside Ravenna.
      The cold, polished wall

fixes something deathly here,
   but of stone not flesh.
      Nothing of the fecund earth

holding Shelley and Keats,
   their good friend Severn,
      Hardy's singers of that shadowy wall

and history-haunted street.
   Inscription. Gold flake and black marble.
      This little formal room,

the purple ghost of Dante
   for those not superstitious
      that hovers here

among the four worlds we inhabit.

BELOW KEATS'S ROOM,
FIRST LIGHT

after Wilbur

I won't forget
standing at the foot of that long marble stair
watching the window where Severn, in silhouette,
tossed the meal Keats rejected—perhaps his last fair

act of criticism as he lay damp
and longing for Fanny Brawne's face,
his young black lungs filling, the light of the lamp
aglow in his room. No one was in that place,

the square had only the fountain sound, some mist,
and no trace of the unacceptable meal. *Toss it*
Keats called weakly to the friend he already missed.
In the Piazza di Spagna, at that hour, I heard Keats say it.

[FROM *Tango*]

POUND

It was a night one might have expected
of Venice:
mid-December, mid-Sixties,
a vaporetto
heading for Accademia—
I was looking for a cheap meal.
It hadn't stopped raining all week
and it was cold,
the dampness above the water
about the same as in,
although there was a little human warmth
in the cabin
where I sat watching the landings
interrupted by the ancient villas
float past the fogged windows—
ghostly, routine, and cold.
It seemed to me, at twenty, like the 19th century,
and I must have written as much
on the pad I kept
in my army surplus jacket.
The light, the sense of history
at night in winter
when time takes on mobility,
the weather rough, unamiable,
made the ride uncomfortable but important.
An old man next to me
watched as I tried to elaborate
the experience. Placing my hand
over the words of descriptive prose
set out in obsessive syllabics,
I looked over at him.
It was Gaudier-Brzeska's portrait of Pound

that prefaces *Personae*
with the eyes colored in,
steady and there.
Not knowing what to say I asked him
what came to mind. I asked him
if he spoke English.
The eyes, blue, humorous and bored,
looked at me a moment.
Nope, he said
in perfect American,
keeping it simple.

NIGHTWORK

The humid night has thrown
against its dark wall
a fistful of fireflies

that snap on and die,
are born again elsewhere
in the line of small trees

growing off the slopes
over Harpswell Bay.
They are fishing for herring

with nets that enclose
this part of the bay.
The sounds of the fishermen

are close—they are setting out
their nets, the engines
starting up, turning off,

the voiced interrogative *Bill?*
I awaken in the dark
not from dream or the stopped,

heavy night, but to their work,
their sounds of such clarity
they could be in this room—

as if they are not on the water at all,
but part of my sleeplessness,
like a radio left on during a night

of fitful sleep, or the presence
of a passing but important intimacy
that makes constant sleep so difficult.

.

Out in the yard at three,
partly asleep
during the lunar eclipse,

I watch the stationed boats and trees
go out a shade at a time
under the pinched wafer.

The colorless day lilies
collapse around me,
their scent growing keener

under the darkened nickel,
hole-in-the-sky,
one-eye rolled up for once,

and only the backup summer
constellations to provide
the muted light above me.

.

Now to wake into the morning,
the body of bay stitched
with herring nets,

herons at water's edge,
the house a cupboard
of damp wood holding

a few earthly treasures.
Here in this room
there's a bay

[FROM *Tango*]

on which I've slept out
another story to find myself
askew in the wash

of early light,
the water again ironed
under a gull's flight.

An armada of peaceful boats
slides on a line
into the channel beyond

the far point,
the sails a unified color
of white light.

                .

There is an island not far from the point
where the mainland gives out.
A woman lives there,

on the leeward side,
her well up a path feet deep
with the deciduous spoilage

of the island trees
and nothing else
but the layered rocks

studded with black quartz
that abut the ocean,
the thousand gulls

and two fish hawks
that nest in the tree
above the well.

Outside her glassed-in kitchen
there is a great deal
of weather to consider,

the attending light,
the wildlife
active on the water surface.

At sundown the insects rise
to irritate the air
and our participation

in the sensible passing
into night. We start
the fire and evening meal.

It is what we say now—
the water breaking down
outside, the body of island

endlessly dark—that gets taken
back to the mainland. Tonight
we share the hundred true things.

.

One day I'll give up this piece of land
over the water, backed by pines
and minor fields,

bullied by the sand and salt wind.
And once gone,
there'll be no need

to return to the fish spine
and bay rock, to the skittish
lobster that scuttles

[FROM *Tango*]

beneath the Whaler
and later lends its shell
to the sea brine, the coastal

wash-up, the tidal scar
that's momentary but recurring.
Perhaps years from now, and miles,

it will be possible to recall
this land, the dark subjugating
nights attached to the coast here.

.

Farther north I had a friend
who sat in a chair by the window
thinking over his own geography:

the refined English lawn,
the surf on his serrated rock-beach,
and the island, barely visible, beyond,

matte on the reflecting skin of summer bay.
Each evening he knew that on another
he would approach the island

and emerge from the water
unalterably changed, indifferent
to his piece of land on the north coast.

.

Leaving is what I take up in the evening.
By morning I have found a way
to stay on another day. The herons

follow the tide up the beach and fly off,
the tide slips back, I take stock.
By evening it is time to leave again.

My friend up the coast
disappeared one night
after a dinner with some people he knew.

They found him a few days later
on his own beach, at the tide mark.
There's not much left but the attempt to stay.

.

I want to protect the day lilies
from the direct light of the sun,
from the storms that flare up

off a calm sea with so little warning
that the summer people are still sunning
when the first unexpected rush of wind

brings on the curtain of rain.
I want the nights to myself,
with no other lamp than my own

illuminating the pages as I turn them,
as the rain turns the still-green
shingles of my house to wine.

I want the memory of this land
in the air when there is only
forest, or flatland, or mountain.

I want this encrusting air to roughen
the surfaces of wherever I find myself,
so when the lights go out up inland roads

there will be again the saline smell of tidal deposits,
the appeased gull-cry calling out,
the ongoing sea-sound in the shell of night.

[FROM *Tango*]

THE SUMMER RENTALS

for my father

Today we went to see the summer rentals
that belong to Mrs. Marian Forster.
Her house, up the road from the Camden marina,
was off to the left, placed on the bay
across from the Curtis Island lighthouse.

She was a talker, with a quick, momentary smile—
you would have likened it to a jab,
but would have liked her handsome good looks.
I thought of you because she had just married
a man she knew in Los Angeles thirty years ago

who was built like you, tall and thin, elegant
in his dark suit and tie. A European with your face,
had you lived long enough, and your good humor
that lived in the eyes. His name was Harry.
Over proper drinks we talked summer rentals

with Mrs. Forster, or Mrs. Someone Else now—
we weren't given Harry's last name.
It was clear from the way he watched her
he was in love for the first time,
or still in love with his first love.

Talking to him was like talking to you.
Although I don't think we spoke of anything
in particular, it was like the talk we had
tossing a ball back and forth outside our house,
or walking down Van Nuys Boulevard.

Mrs. Forster liked us—we were "an interesting couple."
She took Jeanne's face in her hands
and asked me, "Is this a summer thing?"
Mrs. Forster, working the world of possibility,
never lost the spirit of romance.

She showed us, with delicate speed, "the small house,"
in which we could hear the sounds of the bay—
but not as well as in her house, she explained.
The stove in our kitchen had only four burners
and used electric heat, on which she refused to cook,

hers being a Garland with six gas burners
and a salamander, suitable for her style of living.
She told us the guests who lived on her property
had keys to every door, but as we grew silent,
followed with a confirmation that she of all people

believed in the importance of privacy.
I wonder what you would have thought.
Certainly you would have voted against renting,
in spite of being charmed by Mrs. Forster
and her property's flawless situation on the water.

We returned to her house and the women wandered off
to look at other rooms, pieces of furniture,
photographs of the second wedding and of her first husband,
who seemed someone rarely referred to in that house.
Harry and I talked a bit about his work in California,

his new life with Mrs. Forster, and he even explained
that when Mr. Forster died he had arrived to take her
"out of the woods." I knew he was Swedish
by the quick intake of breath that occurred when I said
something he agreed with. His sidelong glance and smile

[FROM *Tango*]

presented the one context we could share.
It seemed to me, as we talked, that he knew
I was talking to you.
It was his eyes that allowed me to imagine asking
the two or three things I've wanted to ask you.

As we left, knowing it would be impossible to return,
I remembered the first room I rented, against your better judgment,
as well as the room where I last saw you. I shook Harry's hand.
It was large and dry and surprisingly strong. As strong,
I returned the handshake you taught me as a boy.

EPITHALAMIUM

In the streets the crowds go about their business
like they always do here, in the rain, or in the clear
cold mornings before the shops close for the midday.

It is possible to do nothing but participate outside
along with everyone else, to look through the glass
and imagine unwrapping what is perfectly displayed.

They have lit small oil lamps the entire length
of the Via di Ripetta, where our rooms are ready for you.
The only information you need now is to know

that the walls are salmon-colored and there are carpets
to make the mornings easier to negotiate. The kitchen
is serviceable—enough for coffee and good toast.

We'll walk through the city that is so familiar to us:
the Caravaggios in San Luigi and the Piazza del Popolo,
and the *trattorie* sprinkled like *parmigiano* over the city.

I have alerted the notaries and the witnesses,
the officials at the Campidoglio and the embassy,
and the offices that will ask if there is anything

that speaks against what we're about to do. Even
the gold bands have been located in Via della Croce—
the time has come. I am waiting for you.

Rome
December, 1982

[FROM *Tango*]

NAMING THE UNBORN

Marry late and the next question
concerns children.

Who doesn't want a child
before they are taken away?

Of a sleepless night
I've imagined a girl,

myself a devoted but strict,
adoring father.

To call her by name now
could be bad luck,

although my superstitions
are easily overcome:

a piece of paper
in the absence of wood. I call her

by her hundred names,
touch wood,

and await what will come,
this vigil we keep for the nameless.

WALKING IN THE 15TH CENTURY

There are angels on the road from San Sepulcro
to Monterchi, and olive trees;
there are grapevines that bring forth
the Umbrian wine Piero drinks
before he goes back
to his pregnant Madonna and the women
attending her. She too will travel this road,
but long after we've gone.

The 15th-century sun is up and to us
it seems *youthful*. It seems *uncomplicated*.
There are angels on the road,
or perhaps they remind us of angels
we've seen on the old canvases
five hundred years later. The air
this time of year feels strict,
the leaves, early autumn, fugacious.

Sometimes, if the distance is not too great,
it is possible for the unborn
to walk with us. Perhaps they are the angels.
Piero might have experienced his Madonna's child,
destined through his art to remain
in utero forever, in this way.
My daughter and I continue along the road;
the wind travels with us.

Piero will have to hurry along to catch us
before we reach the spectral hill town
and the little chapel a kilometer beyond it
that awaits his Madonna.

[FROM *Tango*]

She must be there when I arrive
with the mother of our unborn child
to pay the caretaker the few hundred lire
for a look.

CHILD RUNNING

The little girl runs too quickly in the summer afternoon.
It is late afternoon and she runs along the beach,
   her parents nowhere in sight, no relatives, only
   the waves of the bay repeating alongside her

as she runs the hysterical, off-balance run of children
overly excited, anticipating, dramatic, out of control.
   It might be the small red boat at the end of the bay,
   or the heron following back the tide after herring,

or the group of children playing farther down the beach
with a ball. Something calls to her. As far as
   I'm concerned, there are too many boats alight in the bay,
   too many flying insects. I'm thinking of Marianne Moore's monkeys,

who winked too much, as I stand at night on this lawn looking at the lights
across the water, of her elephants with fog-colored skin
   during the overcast mornings here, of the day's events,
   the tidal movement on the beach, the weather and menus for tomorrow.

Every day there is one less day no matter what you believe,
or in whom. This, of course, discounting the afterlife.
   If you think too much about what there is
   you begin to lose what you have.

This is foreshadowing and it preoccupies me. In my hand
a piece of burnt toast, a grown woman asleep where I left her,
   her body curled around the shape I no longer inhabit.
   On loan, the makeup of what is visible at this hour.

The playing child is one distraction, the warmth of the day another. The layout of the scene below demands attention— it is not a matter of description but of focus. The weather's holding. What's one ecstatic child running on the beach?

WORDS OF ADVICE

Language held you above the water,
you breathed,
you took hold of yourself.
Off the millponds, light
fired the discursive
opportunities of the scene.
You called back
pre-dark dinners as a child
among those of your blood.
Write me,
someone with years of stability
asked of you
as another year turned.
And what was it your mother told you
never to forget?
They've taken away your father
and the little song
you remember him by.
It goes like this. . . .

You called back the young women—
their slender, lonely bodies
stayed awhile at your side,
they said what they had to.
Make it easy on yourself;
there comes a time
when you'll sit down alone,
finished with yet another story,
and begin to assemble
what has been given over to you—
your face remembers
its repertoire of moves

[FROM *Tango*]

and there is a song
that keeps you awake.
A single detail of light
is dragged over the water.
You called back
something you were told
not long before your father's death.
It was a little kindly advice,
surviving on the body of its melody,
the lyrics long ago lost on you.

AMARYLLIS

Far out beyond the forest I could hear
the calling of loud progress . . .
—EDWIN ARLINGTON ROBINSON

Through the city the flocks are led
to their last standing, and we look to John,
not Luke, to understand the other life.
Our lessons begin with what is less beautiful.

As I knelt by the grave of our mother
a storm passed over us, and a harsh rain
snapped the necks of the long-stemmed tuberoses
we brought to honor memory. The rain

passed and left the day without a breeze,
left the humid heat that follows summer rain.
One by one those attending the dead
filed through the mud of the cemetery

until I was left alone, standing there
in the place of stillness. And soon the light
began to fade and there was only
the loneliness of the afterlife that hung

just beyond the sickening scent of unrooted
flowers tightening on their last day.
Around so many dead the ante is one
more indispensable member of the living—

we are to imagine that person here on another day
and to understand how the women and men
who lie here have each been the imagined.
As I stood by this graveside, giving over

[FROM *Tango*]

one of the beloved to the sanctified earth,
a man I hadn't seen touched my arm
and motioned for me to follow him.
Distraught, as he must have been each time here,

he brought me to the one unflowered grave
and placed my hand on the stone with his
wife's name cut into it. And then he dropped
to his knees in the mud and began to rock.

There must have been a brief song to accompany
the palsied hand and opaque eye,
but I heard only the whine of tires
pursuing the expressway,

the water dropping through the trees. I watched him there
as he rocked in the mud and spoke to her without a sound—
with witness he appeared no longer lonely under this
seasonable summer weather. I touched

his little shoulder and he stood up.
His loss meant nothing to me—and mine
nothing to him, not this loss or my losses to come,
not yet finished with the landscape enclosed here.

I remember thinking the man too old
to stand so long like this. He brought no flowers,
hadn't dressed up, didn't know what to say
as we stood there, the knees of his pants

baggy with mud. He hadn't said a word,
but it was his loss that seemed at that moment
the one attended to. Small birds
clouded the air, the hum of evening traffic grew.

[VI]

FOREIGN NEON

FOREIGN NEON

Consider a landscape of winter,
        snow on the hill, ice
    along the roads,
            a fire throwing heat into a room

and blue smoke into low-hung, damp afternoon air.
        But it remains summer here
    in the foothills
            and you've grown sleepy, tired

of so many endless afternoons
        with only a book and glass
    of mediocre wine, what's local
            here. You've said well

what you have to say and have given over
        what you have to give.
    You like to think there's something endless
            in what's still to be discovered.

Consider distance, other locations, long flights
        to high-contrast cities
    lit-up at night in foreign neon.
            Will it be enough?

She wakened you out of inventive dreaming,
        took a cool cloth to your head,
    brought to the room
            this glass of cool water?

And what do you dream here Mr.
    Domestic, living the life
   as if this life were something rustic,
      more than just one time around?

This isn't a dress rehearsal,
    your mother said, quoting
  from one rustic source or another.
     You dream the habitable dreams,

you dream the dream of co-habitation,
    one good woman, one address,
  a life worth repeating day by day.
     And the glass of cool water?—

it comes to room temperature and remains
    untouched, leaving a colorless ring
  on the wormwood nightstand, the woman's
    face in shadow, one hand

on the white sheet, looking deeply into the inevitability
    of her future, the rising sun
  tattooing the noticeably smooth surface of
    her cheek, a color akin to foreign neon.

[FROM *Foreign Neon*]

METAPHYSICAL

Yes, I thought this to be everlasting,
no not waking up, no break of day
not blazing forward out of due east:
blue skies or grey, rain or shine.
I heard the recognized voices
rise attached to the scents of breakfast
to call me down to the new day.
I lived on the coast, tidal, scented
by the submerged inhabiting the shore. Bones
of the no longer swimming, flesh of darkness
de-shelled, isolated, laid out. The rotting
and the called back, what we call ebb and flow.
It's preserving the continuation of flow that keeps us
awake during the hours of darkness, afloat,
buoyant till come-what-may, isn't that it?—
what's merely ongoing, nothing more abstract.
We weep unnerved for what doesn't blink awake.
Oh yes, how the world rises before us
and goes by.

PROTECT YOURSELF

for one accused of selfishness

Outside, a feckless day occurs,
the light of a clarity
that lights a hundred objects
you've never noticed, expressions
of passersby where only blankness
struck you before. There are officers
to guide you, signs and announcements,
the sound of traffic pressing up
and downtown according to the tides
of the tri-colored traffic lights.
And out of sight members of the family:
the immediate family and the once removed,
and then the informal population
who from time to time get close to you.
You can't worry all the time
about loss, unannounced departures,
resignations of those whose presence
may still be required.

                        There are animals
who can enter and in time inhabit
your interior life. Which is to say
you begin to dream
they acquire language, take on sexuality,
and lead secretive second-lives:
bank accounts, political connections
with the wrong party, strangers who enter
the feeding process, followed
by the actual hours of early morning
abandonment. And finally the dream
of losing them arrives, even if you find
substitutes to stand in for what's irreplaceable,

[FROM *Foreign Neon*]

so that something is always there
for you, and if you've protected yourself
you step to the side
and don't bear the full weight
of unresolvable loss. Make yourself
an aficionado of massive denial and live
a casual life (routine, repetition, parade),
counter whatever gets tossed your way—
safe conduct through it all—
and as we live numbered days, believe
there's safety in numbers
when you remember the number's one.

INFIDELITIES

I.

I read somewhere that every love
has its own government. Or was it
that every love has
the government it deserves?
What is ours?
The heat of August is thick,
an unwoven blanket of air,
damp, present and persistent.
Here, we two representatives
half-sleep some place half-known,
remembered
in moments of utter distraction,
but never in despair.
Before we depart, gain again
our former lives, we might
for the sake of transition
gaze a few moments
at the adjacent apartment house at dusk,
each window a single friendly frame
of others nearly like us, caught
in a life carried on
without the negotiations of duplicity.
We take up the habit
of referring to others
in the third person once-removed,
while for us there's only
the everlasting present: we walk out
into the general evening and you say
it's like walking out
of a deeply engaging matinee:

[FROM *Foreign Neon*]

so much sudden light,
so much going on,
so much of what came before
still residing in us.
Is the frantic siren
playing our song?
You nearly say what we're committed
to saying never, the understood unsaid—
even here there are laws and rights
to protect the guilty,
even if the jury's always in.
Our penalty,
with conviction or without:
life sentences
back-to-back.

2.

There's a grey cat who's not allowed into the house
where our cat for twenty years has been the one cat.

There's a storm working over the low mountains,
building with a stillness of air and light

over the nearest peaks. And soon the rain,
the full storm gets underway, thunder and light,

the passing thickness of air, the sudden rush
of wind, and the sheet of rain spraying the valley.

The grey cat presses against the door frame, and we sit
down to dinner, our cat in the third chair, the stew

done right and placed on the table, the wine poured.
The evening survives the storm and we walk out for a look

at what's left. A moon finally free, a hostage
sprung from a jihad of clouds breaking up. The wet grass

regains its starch from this afternoon's wet heat,
and the grey cat emerges from under the porch steps,

dry but intense, charging our legs and getting over
in the language of cats her wish to enter our lives.

In the window, mirroring the table lamp, our cat,
shrewd, disappointed, and accusatory, studies us.

She's hurt and shows no apparent sympathy for a sister
left to the cold of the outside world. We're not surprised,

she's an indoor cat, her claws clipped, her movements
suited to the angles of furniture, the surface of rugs.

She will stand before her bowl of food and demand our best,
a gourmet cat when hungry: squab, fillet, hearts of chicken.

3.

Adjoining suites in cities halfway round the world.
Flowers for your room or mine?—we are all of us
so thoughtful by distance, by way of longing
known only to those left what once was shared, shared
dailiness. The sun sets in Malaysia, comes up
in Malawi, sets again almost anywhere. There's local beer
in Srinagar, dangerous fish to consume at gold prices
in Tokyo, dishes spiced with ground cumin
along the North African coast—part of the experience.

Don't forget postcards: Etc., Love, . . .
Don't eat salads east of the Mediterranean;
in general, leave the uncooked to local consumption.

[FROM *Foreign Neon*]

For the last night there's suddenly a balcony,
a table set for one, mirrored by an adjoining table,
set for one, a vase of flowers each, a flinty white
from Chablis, a napkin bleached and starched stiff. Two,
under whatever local weather can manage. To departure!
To one more long flight back. To the airline's pressed meat.
To the whimsy of airport control. To the profound
second-rate paperback novel whose hapless characters
in their tireless sprint around the track of love
will accompany you the full distance home.

4.

We talked in the oyster bars
and on the streets the homeless
entertained us, dancing or singing,
clowning for the homeowners, hats out,
hands out, moving.
                    Strolling
is what we do here, destination
left for later. And later we're somewhere dark,
the music higher, off the street,
an arena of candlelit tables, black leather
actors playing the role of waiters
and bad wine poured out of unmarked jugs
which we drink with impunity.

There are those listening to music,
those trading one practiced gesture for another.
Where do we go from here? The set's ended
and the food begins to arrive at the tables.

Back on the street it's late, dangerous
if you read the papers or listen to the cabbies.
There's a moon hung up there but it's soiled.
There are stars too somewhere, but hidden

behind this air, thick with accrual—of
everything about life in this town.
We can talk away by one body of water or another,
the evening's finished and we are like all things here,
strangers like everyone, without destination,
parting with nothing left to say.

5.

There's a rich, humid park that carries on for acres.
It might be placed downtown, or simply midtown,
in a large, unknowable midwestern city, near a lake
whose native game fish draw those with time on their hands
from both East and West. Chartered boats, guides,
rented gear to fit the tall and short, the hip and guileless.

The two of us meet Wednesday afternoons there,
beneath hundred-year-old oaks that on sunny days toss shade
no less than a hundred feet. We meet there with blankets
and a bag of prepared lunch. The city sirens that work
the periphery of the park sing with care what we like to call,
simply, *our song*. We sip our wine, we mouth the lyrics

of what needs to be everlasting. We note what wants attention:
our careful dress, the casual play of hair and percentage
of color in the other's complexion, blood at the surface—
with superior attention we begin to understand the face
looking back, filled with expression, looking for the necessary
translation, required understanding. On the sea

it's red sky at night, sailor's delight—buoys, red
right returning. Simple indications. Our damp hands,
finally freed, mean business if we allow the passing on
of substance. We'll look for signs in the agates of vision,
peepholes into the deep emotional stations we call our hearts.
Not even the storm forming overhead will drive us back.

[FROM *Foreign Neon*]

Not even the inclement work of weather will defeat the good purpose
of this afternoon. A freight train pulls a hundred Chryslers
up the hill we've yet to coin a name for, claim as one more
possession, one more part of the memory—we with little else
than an afternoon to spare in the sparse post-storm light.
We want it this lingering way: constant renaming, constant return.

TIDAL

I walk out at sunset, over the prehistoric beach slate,
coming down behind the tide, the mussels gasping still,
the seaweed just breathing. It's fresh, brilliant cool
rolling the air, a sound of leafage taking the wind.

The air tonight is what Dante would have wished for
rising from his dark journey through the endless nights
of our poor human soul. Coastal, tainted with fish kill,
pine tar, the olfactory avatars of the tides.

The sun gone over the fluttering trees, the moon just up
released from the European shore: the givens. Room only
for one to feel out what's still ahead. In darkness
my solitude fits like fabric, tailored to last forever.

[FROM *Foreign Neon*]

LEAVING THE CITY

We were complaining about the streets,
how there were none left
whole, and the general disrepair
of everything the eye
cared to consider.

We were complaining about those
abandoned to the streets,
their mobile homes, and the window-
washers on the street corners
who muddied the clear windows
of our cars. And of course
we recognized the pure danger here
for what it is and placed it
high on our list of complaints.

We said we had to leave.

We said there was no reason
to undergo what daily the city
placed before us,
on our dish, as it were,
the undeniable diminishing
returns. Our politics
made it impolitic to hate
the helpless, the homeless,
or the enemies of our well-being—
and the mayor refused to engage
in meaningful dialogue,
thinking only to give over
his problems to us

with the single exception
of his carefully selected wardrobe.

We wondered how we had stayed,
if we might have overstayed
and now there was no getting out.

We felt the energies pulse through us,
the need to respond
to the five million messages
passing through lines
of communication to the waiting
services of private answering equipment.

We felt love dissipate
in the humidity of the city summer,
the longing for real life
at a moderate pace—
well, just the greenery of out-of-town,
the casual, easy-going *good* day.
And finally, as the electrical sun
weakened on its dimmer,

we wept openly for our exhaustion.

[FROM *Foreign Neon*]

ARGUMENT

But it ate a hole in my heart,
she said when I complimented her
on the use of restraint, so useful
in the ongoingness of shared life,
life at the midpoint, where we are.

We note how even the offspring of friends
frankly worry about their own aging.
We note the second generation
of pets, whose kidneys have already
begun to fail, their balance fading,

giving up the body's tension.
What did I say to establish
that tension in our bodies?
Did she just give in for the sake
of a good night's sleep, nothing countered

to keep us up and at it, to turn
over what's been tossed often enough?
Her fair head's an aquarium
of trouble, troubling through troubled sleep.
The cost? One more entry through the heart.

CLUMSY GRATITUDE

There is only one secret despite the many
the lovers can tell each other. One secret,
dark and white—white
as lies are white, dark, as those thoughts
never uttered to the other. Duration
provides the subtext for what can be
easily presumed, as in *expectation*.
As in *I expected more from you*, as in
I didn't expect this from you.

                     And later,
holding his wife without clothes or blankets
on the bed stripped for the maid,
he won't mention the dark green dress
she wore to greet him at the door,
the darker pattern that emerged like a print
just beginning to come forward
in a darkroom tray. She had sat across from him
in that dress he had so often admired,
had so often told her so. Was she telling him
the truth? And what was this little flurry
of trust? He couldn't be convinced she was
saying anything about the truth. What had happened?
Sympathy, possibly something even stronger?
Her shoulders seemed so thin, so frail and available,
turned in upon themselves as if recently
pulled forward in embrace. What he remembers.

And now his wife on the stripped bed, cooling
in the late night, both of them slightly high
from the red wine, the dizzying understanding
of what comes next, what stretches ahead.

[FROM *Foreign Neon*]

They sleep and dream out what they live.
And the other woman, her green dress over a chair,
her shoulders now laid back in sleep.
The moon is at stake. The waves tumble in.
There is a song that has all this, the story
this story, however and by whomever it is told.
Yes. Only together can they know
in what ways the secret revealed
is nothing more than an ongoing form of grace.

COFFEE

There was a little coffee house in the mid-Sixties, placed halfway through Laurel Canyon, in Los Angeles. There was a woman who lived in the canyon with her small girl. I can't remember their names, twenty-five years ago, but it occurs to me that little girl is now thirty, perhaps with a child of her own. Quickly it's possible to look back and find yourself out far enough the land you so recently left is no longer in sight. The room where we slept that summer was screened-in, a porch really, set on the edge of woods. In the morning the little girl joined us until her mother got up to make coffee. She was the first woman I knew in that way with a child. We drove everywhere, the three of us, one family just driving—on our way. What she taught me during the long nights that summer, screened-in with the low whimper of wind floating down through the canyon, the casual closeness of that time, the mornings following, are just part of everything else. Sometimes, after she'd fall asleep, I'd walk to the café with a book in my pocket and some change for coffee. And then I'd walk home, late, the air hollow, flower-filled, the thought of her asleep enough. It wasn't possible. Coffee is the drink of the office, of insomniacs and lovers. She is so far removed now that I'm thinking of her. It was an easy passion, brief, thoughtful, even *passionate*. A few years ago I drove by the café, a garage now, and where I remembered her house to be. I parked the car and walked up the long ladder of stairs to the gate I painted dark brown one early day in mid-August. There was no one home, but I wouldn't have rung the bell anyway— that little girl would have been her mother's age the last time I saw her. The house bore small resemblance to my memory—it had grown ornate, the gate repainted white, shutters added and painted a cheerful teal, the garden gouged out of the earth behind the room that was once screened-in, now part of a two-story addition. Why should anything have remained? And my last thought before turning back down the steps was our last meal together. We ate in bed, a curried chicken she taught me to make, rice and a little date chutney she'd made for house gifts. And before I left we made love with consider-able nostalgia, as if this last act were itself an act of memory recalled late in the dead of some night years and an age later, the book put aside, the cups of coffee cooling, just out of reach.

LAST DANCE

You were dancing.
You were dancing
but without music,
although the music played,
tunes
that would have
reminded you
death once seemed
so very far away.
You spent entire nights
adding on your fingers
how many more times
you could live again
your ten years
before reaching seventy.
Six more lifetimes—
six more times around
the short block
you'd already run.
And even then it seemed
so short a time,
with so much
still ahead
clouding the future
with one mystery
or another.
But you were dancing,
her head
sending you
dark scents of hair,
the outer ring
of her ear part

[FROM *Foreign Neon*]

of your peripheral vision.
Years of dancing
told you
her eyes were lightly
closed, tapping out
the little light left
in the room of dancers
with spinning globes
of reflected light,
the bass a heart
between your hearts.
Of the seven lives
you granted yourself,
you'd now used four,
addition no longer
required. You thought
living to forty
was luck
and everything after
what we call *gravy*.
And here you are,
lucky but forty nonetheless,
counting what remains
but not with fingers—
what one friend
called the collapse
of the body biology,
sure signs, the reddening
of leaves out of deep summer,
the level road
that suddenly turns
uphill. She's asleep standing,
her fingers dead weight
in your hand, her head
beyond music,
listening to *your* music.
That's right, you

were dancing
without music in music,
the years rolling
off the lasting
remembered melodies.
You were dancing a slow dance,
but you were dancing.

DAYBREAK

The angular,
stick-legged walk
of the bay's heron
is what dawn
spawns at the rim
of receding water.
It walks like a cat
walking on water:
outraged, cautious,
regular as it places
one foot back
into the tide, lifting
the other, and so on
down the encrusted beach.
The symbol of sun
becomes sun in a moment,
shedding the husk
of imagined sun
which begins to beat
in some other dark
like a night moth
against a screen,
with the changing temperatures
of the sea-wind blowing
across those who lie
in the bleached gauze of
summer sleep.
What else of the dawn?
The interrogative *Bill?*
from the lobster boat
whose family pots dot

our water-yard.
The exclamatory birdsong.
The explosive light breaking
off bay glass.

[FROM *Foreign Neon*]

DEAD BIRDS

All the days you can remember
of childhood,

looking through the window
at birds

feeding in the damp grass.
The first days you can remember

after childhood,
through the window of a car

parked at some hermetic sunset,
the birds feeding in the ocean

from the air over the sand cliffs.
And what's close enough at hand

that memory hasn't figured yet,
the scene unfolding here,

the scattered, noisy sea-birds
over some summer back bay,

farther north and east
than might have been imagined.

The birds hold their own on down-drafts
to the sea-surface, riding back up

the air's salt-tides where the patterns
of submerged fish appear

before dropping, rushing their catch.
They survive suspended

and in this way are remembered,
brought back into play

as part of the plain past.
But they die as secretly as we,

no bodies in the evening grass,
found rarely even on a forest's edge

or the rocks of this eastern coast.
Where do birds die? the child

in the woods asks as she and her mother
unwrap sandwiches composed

the evening before.
The mother looks up

and the sun looks back,
studious, waiting.

And the birds roll down the invisible
threads that net the fine, high air

of their traffic—the sun above, the small
questioning girl and her mother about to eat—

as if gravity likes what flies less
and so abandons the hollow-boned

and marrow-free to remain tied
to the woman and child

[FROM *Foreign Neon*]

committed to this land.
But the residents of air return,

like a ball along its arc, birds
remembered or forgotten, as if gravity

could care, but to die—*where?*
the little girl asks again, the sun

turned red on the late angle, the woman
at last responding with a probable list:

caught in the highest branches
of old trees, dropped over deep water,

over mud-flats, swamps,
parts of the forest

where there is no need
to go—this is how they disappear.

And what awaits these fallen bodies
are the commas of the earth, climbing

through the beak, the eyes and genitalia
to reduce these bodies of air

from the inside, emerging
from the soft, land-bound blanket

of feathers back into the air, the bird-
spirit like memory rising, gravity free.

SUMMER IN THE MIDDLE CLASS

All over America
it's suddenly
mid-July
We're chasing
our sons around
the yard
with balls and sticks
We are lumbering
because we are overweight
and a little older
being survivors
of the baby boom
making good the legacy
At sundown
a million barbecues ignite
as if from a single match
Webers
Crestlines
international hibachis
and the sad slabs of meat
begin to emerge
from their various marinades
The tables get set
and the mosquitoes awaken
for the evening meal

When they have finished
what is rightfully theirs
the children are removed
from the tables
and the adults open
another bottle or can of beer

[FROM *Foreign Neon*]

The evenings are special
this time of year
the heat finally bearable
the coals a coolish grey
dying into themselves
It's what happens in unison
that makes America America
the lights going off
the fluorescent show
of t.v. coming on
and then
the total darkness

CANDLES FOR BESSIE

We walk as far as we can
and the 15th Century still shows up
at every corner. In the canvases
that hang in the cool sanctuaries of the church

the members of the highest family find themselves
revealed in the infinite postures of holding.
Again and again you walk to the darkest corner
and take a candle from the stack of votives.

The coins you've saved drop with a noise
into the offering box and the prayer is made.
The wick catches fire
in the muted, dusty light of late afternoon.

When we begin back your candles are burning
on the seven hills. Vespas slice the evening air.
Because the Romans don't always believe in sidewalks
there's never enough room to walk without caution.

It's the hour of swallows.
It's the hour when the citizens begin to walk.
And all over the city your twenty prayers
throw light against the darkening vestibules.

[FROM *Foreign Neon*]

STAZIONE

1. *Blue, Arrival*

She arrives but isn't met because her lover
lost the time of her arrival. The blue air
of late autumn carries her to the gate,
where she turns over her first-class ticket stub
to the mute at the ticket window. When he looks up
he sees the cobalt stone balancing her middle finger,
the blue cast of the pearls that reflect the vein-light
of the blood's own round trip, and then the loss,
her companion on that long journey back.

2. *Citrus*

The prettiest woman in the station isn't traveling.
She releases the scent of the tangerine she scratches
while waiting for the last train to enter its stall.
Beneath the wooden bench where she waits, the thin peel.

3. *Waiting*

The waiter in the cafe insists on serving them tea
with his hook, which he does with considerable dexterity.
And when they agree to lemon, he inserts the hook
into one of the freshly cut halves and lets the juice
flow into the cups. In the mirror, hung high
in one of the corners of the room, they see the waiter
walk to the far end of the bar and, when he thinks
he's not being observed, smell the beak of his hook.

4. *The Mute*

He goes late to the station for the evening paper
and she follows him home. She knocks on his door
after he locks it. She wears the sweeper's blue
uniform, hired by the state in one of its gestures
of good intent. He pulls back the sheet of his bed
and gets in. The knocking continues and the wind
works the telephone wires as he raises
the newspaper: 10,000 jobs created for the unemployed,
new aid for the homeless. Good gesture.
He pulls up the blankets and turns out the light.

5. *Message*

He goes late to the station for the evening paper.
As he searches for small change he hears his name
called out over the loudspeaker, giving the track
of his departure. It is verified with a silent nod
by the woman selling papers in the dark kiosk.

6. *Blue, Departure*

She places her hand in the leather purse she carries
and removes a piece of white tissue, which she crushes
and returns to her purse. His hands remain
in the pockets of his trousers.
She returns her hand to the purse. He places his arm
on the wall above her head and leans forward.
From the purse she removes the small dark pistol.
From the purse she removes the silver knife.
From the purse she removes a blue handkerchief
to collect the moisture that has amassed
in the corners of her eyes. He takes her by the shoulder
and lets her go. The nearest track is hers.

[FROM *Foreign Neon*]

GONE

after Holan

A girl I didn't know handed me a letter and went away.
But it was many years ago, my hair
was full still, and dark, and I walked without a limp, straight
up, looking ahead for what was yet to come.
She came to my table, kneeled in the sawdust
in front of me, set the envelope on my knees,
then stood up and walked out. The handwriting,
in English, was as delicate as the one blue vein
beating at her temple—as she faced the door I saw only
the left side of her face. I no longer remember
what she wore, and she said nothing. She was not someone
I had seen before, although in front of me she looked
familiar, but in a distant way, as if we had been close
informally on the street, or in line at a tram stop.
What the letter said and if it was meant for me
is not important. But I have carried this story
for these many years—lean, fat, indifferent—in spite of
the clever play memory brings to bear as I look back to it.
We were young men traveling through northern cities.
We drank the local beer and smoked meerschaum pipes,
tossed literature around the table like a softball.
August, the nights were endless, like the constellations
of the young men and women we were that year,
the year everyone wore jeans and T-shirts dyed
a faded sky-blue—combinations that dissolved
quietly under the influence of beer and our own bodies
into the slightly-darkened northern night,
hand in hand, with only the simple in mind.
What the letter said memory has long since rewritten.
I have sent out my letters stamped and well-addressed,
but they are not returned.
I know she's been dead a long time,
the blue vein a river through her golden temple at rest.

HALFWAY

Chekhov said if you wish to have
a little spare time, do nothing.
So we begin doing nothing,
but find nothing's work as soon as
we abandon ourselves to it,
to nothing, released at sunrise
from the pull of what must come next.

Memory rushes in to fill
the sudden loss of momentum,
the willed standstill we now approach.
Doing nothing there's equal time
for what's taken place already,
for the nothing happening now.

Or, just work toward a single end
to achieve what you think you want—
repeating over and over
what it is you believe you do best.
Chekhov said of his friend Pavel,
*He cooked for forty years; he loathed
the things he cooked and never ate.*

[FROM *Foreign Neon*]

HOUSE OF FLAME

1.

Get the marinade right.
Bathe the ingredients
for the proper duration
and remove immediately.
Pat dry, set aside.
The sky is skeletal,
late winter, too cold
for walking into the fields,
the frozen blades of grass
momentary toothpicks.
Overhead a migration,
but in or out of season?
The ice cuts deep
through the lake water,
the wok oil ready to smoke—
everything, ready to soften.

2.

Gather your knives, sharpen with care.
Gather your vegetables, dice with care.
Decide on the cooking oil, select with care.
Heat your wok over a high flame, with care
for such fire and the heating oil. With care
add the vegetables but consider hunger
as restraint, cooking as desire. With care.

3.

The sea's in a state,
tossed, worried to a frenzy
of white ridges and dark hollows
rushed headlong to the rocks.
The heat of the last days
of summer has drifted out
into another system of weather.
There's a young woman who's
wandered down the beach, her shoes
bleached mauve, her hair just dark.
Behind me the wok oil trembles,
overheated, anticipatory—no, looking
for the still untouched, delicate
surface of cubed daikon, the exposed flesh
of sliced duck, the smashed
cloves of garlic that enter
the night after sleep to keep us
in good luck—fire,
animal, vegetable and stones
to receive the tide.
In the sink the damp wooden sticks
still tossing the evening meal, there's
ice in the glass of water
on the nightstand, to drink
anticipating the rising
sun.

4.

On the counter two white teacups,
a wooden-handled cleaver
handed down from another generation.
This configuration suggests
emptiness.

[FROM *Foreign Neon*]

On the cutting board a line
of cut vegetables, the work
of someone married to clarity.

On the kitchen wall a list
of ingredients for another meal,
the hand clear, black ink,
a list of ten items,
nothing abbreviated, nothing
left out.

On the table a new set
of chopsticks, their wrapping
wrinkled and dropped
carelessly nearby.
Maybe a letter, too,
with a foreign postmark,
unopened.
Beyond now the hour of eating,
the moon, a plug of rice
held with care in the window,
throws a white shroud.

On the floor near the bed
two plates, the vegetables
gone from one,
on the other cool now,
their white, green and purple skins
wrinkled.

5.

Your white plate of white fish
is flesh and clay
no longer—one given
over to the air, the other

to the breakage of settlement,
change and exchange.
One day your meal, the next
a spectacle of memory,
arbitration, the miracle
of survival.

6.

She said without thinking,
without thinking too deeply
or thinking too deeply,
Do you need to be drunk?
Was there even a thread
of ambiguity drawn
upon that lovely face,
spiced as it was by the hour?
Well, they may have been dancing,
or just finishing
on a song from their
early days as individuals,
her look simultaneously
transparent and opaque.

7.

Again, but seven years later,
a full lunar eclipse,
secret passage of the moon
into our shadow, diminishing
for the few hours of its duration
the source of illumination.
For the first half of the eclipse,
as the moon shades and darkens,
we marinate the clear caps

of white field mushrooms.
And with the moon half in shadow
we spin these inner moons of the earth
on the sprigs of fire focused
under the tempered steel of the wok.
They color to the orange of the moon
in full lunar eclipse, which in the air
turns ghostly orange, at once transparent
and opaque as the night wobbles
around it along with twenty million—
not *stars* but *viewers*
who search the altered sky
for a sign, a way to enter
the secret of their own shadow.
But you and I give up that orange note
for this perfect dish of mushrooms,
browned golden in a note of flavored oil
to something transcendent.

8.

From the back room you hear
the cubed chicken dance
in the smoking oil, the beat
of the stirring utensil
slipping through the meat, tossing it
to the sides of the wok, back
to the quivering-hot oil.
From the back room a little smoke.
From the back room the clear scent
of marinade fried into air,
meal scent, on the air notice
of the about-to-appear. Scent
of about-to-begin, to move
from the back room, scent

of the back room,
to the front of the house
where at the table the meal
is as delicate as the lights of cars
passing on the walls, a moment
of brightness within the ongoing night.

9.

With a sharp knife
remove both ends
and cut in half
lengthwise. Wedge out
the hard base knot
and with your fingers
strip off the layers
of burnished skin.
Now is the moment
to cube
with a straight
sure motion the layers
of vegetable.
The pungent white flesh
touching the wok oil
hisses and shakes,
bounces, steams, takes on
the gold cast
of the sun suspended
over the horizon's cool water,
gold of the air just after,
gold of her hair, bleached gold
at the temple, the gold temples.

[FROM *Foreign Neon*]

10.

You were dreaming again, of holding her
in the failing light of some failing
stop-over or another, some merely broken down
town with nothing operative but corruption.
The sun like a cavity filling with blood
on the western horizon
made the ocean Pacific, the late afternoon
dangerous in its willingness to reveal.
Were you dreaming? The warm beer left a ring
on the bamboo where you placed it, a green dress,
moss green, just tossed
over the cane chair, a pale dream
of cloth, abandon, something—what? Your hand
finding for itself a little game with another.
While you were dreaming she walked out to the veranda
wearing your starched white shirt, rolled to the elbows,
the tails down to her knees.
Her feet left small damp marks on the planked floor.
You watched as the light dyed her red,
was she dreaming? In the sink the half-shells
of crustaceans,
three chopsticks and two paper plates.
In the flower pot on the railing she notices
the slender vine-like plant tied with twine
and staked to the clay pot with a chopstick.

11.

Is it possible,
a nervous knife,
vegetables on edge,
is it possible?

An anxious wok,
tentative oil?
The finely chopped daikon
coolly and enviably white.

Yes, hunger as desire,
cool white steam,
the angry snap
of water on oil.

I hear your voice
calling me. Is it
on edge? I'm so
tentative beyond the sound

of your voice, so anxious
all the time. My hand on your arm
inappropriate as linen
where paper is required.

Is it possible?
I remember that evening,
the sheaf of blank paper
just piled, the linen sheets

still starched—stiff,
unyielding, dead white and fragrant
as white sheets—your white voice
in the expectant air, calling me back.

[FROM *Foreign Neon*]

A Note About the Author

Daniel Halpern was born in Syracuse, New York, in 1945 and has lived in Los Angeles, Seattle, New York City, and Tangier, Morocco. He is the author of seven previous collections of poems, the editor of *Antaeus* and The Ecco Press, and a recipient of many grants and awards, including fellowships from the Guggenheim Foundation and the National Endowment for the Arts. Mr. Halpern teaches in the graduate writing program of Columbia University and divides his time between New York City and Princeton, where he lives with his wife and daughter.

A Note on the Type

This book was set on the Linotype in Granjon, a type named in compliment to Robert Granjon, a type cutter and printer active in Antwerp, Lyons, Rome, and Paris, from 1523 to 1590. Granjon, the boldest and most original designer of his time, was one of the first to practice the trade of type founder apart from that of printer.

Linotype Granjon was designed by George W. Jones, who based his drawings on a face used by Claude Garamond (c. 1480–1561) in his beautiful French books. Granjon more closely resembles Garamond's own type than does any of the various modern faces that bear his name.

Composed and printed by
Heritage Printers, Charlotte, North Carolina.
Bound by Kingsport Press, Kingsport, Tennessee.
Designed by Peter A. Andersen